More Praise for *The Inspiration Code*

"Inspirational leadership is an absolute requirement for creating and sustaining high-performing teams. *The Inspiration Code* provides practical and insightful guidance on how to leverage skills like listening and cultivating purpose to create an inspired and engaged workforce. "

—John Sigmon, Chief Human Resources Officer, AARP

"*The Inspiration Code* is a clear, practical guide to communicating in ways that move others to action. We're in a time of unprecedented change, where leaders must communicate enthusiasm, vision, and imagination to energize their teams to take big leaps. If you're a leader who wants to drive change, inspire a team, or simply be a better manager, read this book now."

— Atif Rafiq, Chief Digital Officer and SVP of IT, Volvo

"If we're lucky, we've had inspirational leaders who've invested in us, and helped us to be and do more. We know how critical they are in our own trajectory. *The Inspiration Code* is a guide to paying it forward, by helping all of us to be the type of leader who builds careers and improves lives. This book will light a spark!"

— Carol Seymour, CEO and founder, Signature Leaders

THE

INSPIRATION

CODE

THE
INSPIRATI⊙N
CODE

HOW THE BEST LEADERS
ENERGIZE PEOPLE EVERY DAY

KRISTI HEDGES

AMACOM

AMERICAN MANAGEMENT ASSOCIATION
NEW YORK • ATLANTA • BRUSSELS • CHICAGO • MEXICO CITY • SAN FRANCISCO
SHANGHAI • TOKYO • TORONTO • WASHINGTON, DC

Bulk discounts available. For details visit:
www.amacombooks.org/go/specialsales
Or contact special sales:
Phone: 800-250-5308
Email: specialsls@amanet.org
View all the AMACOM titles at: www.amacombooks.org

American Management Association: www.amanet.org

This publication is designed to provide accurate and authoritative information in regard to the subject matter covered. It is sold with the understanding that the publisher is not engaged in rendering legal, accounting, or other professional service. If legal advice or other expert assistance is required, the services of a competent professional person should be sought.

Library of Congress data is available upon request.

ISBN: 978-0-8144-3789-6
E-ISBN: 978-0-8144-3790-2

About AMA
American Management Association (www.amanet.org) is a world leader in talent development, advancing the skills of individuals to drive business success. Our mission is to support the goals of individuals and organizations through a complete range of products and services, including classroom and virtual seminars, webcasts, webinars, podcasts, conferences, corporate and government solutions, business books, and research. AMA's approach to improving performance combines experiential learning—learning through doing—with opportunities for ongoing professional growth at every step of one's career journey.

10 9 8 7 6 5 4 3 2 1

CONTENTS

To Emery, Smith, and Mike
for the everyday things.

INTRODUCTION

This whole thing began with a light.

And that got me looking for the spark.

But let me back up before I get ahead of myself. For the past decade I've worked as a leadership coach. It's the most rewarding job I can imagine. I work with senior leaders and CEOs at all kinds of companies—from global brands that everyone knows to upstart businesses just making their mark. My job is to help leaders communicate in ways that inspire and motivate others. I help them drive change, set visions, get people excited, and lead teams into the future. I get to work with smart and dedicated people, all over the world, who are at the top of their game and who care deeply. They're making good things happen.

As part of my work, I also write about the concepts that I've seen to be effective, to present them in a practical way for anyone trying to advance a career. No matter the type of organization or level of professional, whether speaking one-to-one or one-to-many, certain behaviors are universal. In 2011, I wrote a book called *The Power of Presence* that got me out there in a more expansive way, delivering workshops and keynotes to all kinds of corporate groups, in lots of different settings. And that's when I began to notice the light.

At the beginning of my talks, as a sort of icebreaker, I asked the audience to think of someone who has inspired them. I wanted to have the participants map this inspiring person back to the attributes of leadership presence in my book to make the concepts relatable. Now, when you speak in public, it would be nice to have a room full of people on the edges of their seats, fully engaged, just waiting for you to begin. But just as often, you're there on the podium at 8:00 a.m. on a Tuesday looking out at a tired group of people, distracted by their phones, who showed up only because they were "voluntold" to do it. They've seen lots of speakers and now they're looking at you to see if you're worth their time.

Hence, my icebreaker: When I introduce this discuss-an-inspirational-person exercise, at first people reluctantly move toward their discussion partners, some with barely stifled *it's-one-of-those-workshops* groans. But then they start talking about the people who have inspired them in their lives. That's when I see it. Almost immediately, people's faces light up. Smiles break out. Hands gesture intently. Eyes shine. There's excitement in their voices.

When I ask if anyone wants to share their stories, hands shoot up. I've heard about first bosses, coaches, parents, colleagues, friends, teachers, managers, CEOs, strangers, family members, direct reports, and co-workers. I've heard stories about everyday occurrences and ones that are unique and memorable. The situations and people vary greatly, but I noticed great similarity in what these inspirational people *did*. And it wasn't anything momentous or grand. The inspirational people mentioned communicated in certain, specific ways that made this kind of light shine in people's faces even decades later.

My curiosity piqued, I began wondering how can we have more of that in our workplaces. What effect would it have? Companies are spending millions of dollars to get inspirational leadership behaviors into organizations, and yet, these efforts fall flat. There has to be a way to get closer to this true inspiration that has a lasting impact on others. And so I embarked on my own research to take a deeper dive into what really inspires others, and to outline the very behaviors—or sparks—that create this kind of enduring, energizing light.

Couldn't we all use more of it? Turns out, all it takes is the right conversation.

THE CONVERSATIONS THAT COUNT

In our lives, we have lots of conversations. We have them one-on-one, in groups, in public settings, in meeting rooms, in auditoriums. We have them at home, at work, at the dentist, in line at the DMV, in the car, on walks, and sitting with a beer in the backyard. Nearly all of these conversations flit in and out of our consciousness. We barely remember them.

But every once in a while, we have a conversation that changes our lives. You know the kind. It feels different. It crackles with energy. It has a zing. It makes time stop. Deeper and more real, it lands just right. After we walk away, we're not quite the same as we were before. These are conversations that change how we think about ourselves, that open our minds to what we're capable of doing and show us what's possible. They infuse us with hope, determination, and confidence. They lift our mood, bringing joy and lightness. They fuel our ambition, validate our current choices, or inspire us to make new ones. These aren't ordinary conversations, but conversations that count. They're inspiring and unforgettable. They marinate. We save them in the recesses of our minds. We recount them from time to time. We carry them around like talismans to fortify us for days, months, or our entire lives.

When people describe those who inspire them, they talk about these conversations that count. They're the right words by the right person at the right time. Those who inspire might not even realize what they've done. And yet, look what they've done.

Looking at my own story, I can precisely map the conversations that inspired my decisions and shaped who I became.

I grew up in a small factory town in West Virginia. It was literally gritty, with a limestone quarry in the middle of the town that deposited grit on our cars, outside our windows, and in the bottom of glasses of water. It was a town where people felt lucky to land factory jobs that came with decent wages and guaranteed pensions. Almost 40 percent of my high school class didn't make it to senior year.

We were a family that got by. No extras, with clothes on layaway and groceries that were thin by month's end. Money dictated every decision. The first person in my family to go to college, I had a limited understanding about what a college education required. I didn't know how to choose a major, or even what I could become beyond the few professional occupations, such as doctors and lawyers, that I saw in our town. Statistically, I was a long shot.

But I did make it. I put everything I had into my education, went to Virginia Tech on student loans, and got a full scholarship to Purdue University for graduate school. I learned how to network, and right out of school got a rare, well-paying job in politics that put me in the midst of the most powerful people in Washington. I worked hard and went into corporate life, eventually taking a huge risk by starting a technology-focused communications firm when I was just twenty-eight years old. Ten years later, I sold my stake in the firm, and took another gamble by following a growing passion for leadership: I started a coaching firm to work with senior executives. By following this path, I was able to get two books published and grow a thriving business that challenges and excites me every day.

While I certainly don't claim to be anyone else's image of success, my eighteen-year-old self couldn't even have dreamed this big. I feel exceedingly lucky and grateful to be where I am, with an engaging career, a meaningful life, and a wonderful family around me. And here's why I share this: When I look back, every major move I've made has been preceded by an inspiring conversation. They were conversations that helped me see possibilities, gave me confidence, uncovered my potential, validated my instincts, propelled me forward, and sometimes guided me in making a sharp left turn. People on the other end included:

- My mother and stepmother who listened gently and helped me see my own ability to solve problems as I navigated toward adulthood.

- A few special teachers, who spent time with me between classes and after school, to help me chart a path toward college.

- My church pastor who, in a meeting the summer before college where I proceeded to fall apart over how to afford four years of college, shored up my confidence to keep moving forward.

- An early mentor in politics who met with a young kid who had nothing to offer and showed me what was possible.

- A leader who, upon hearing that I wanted to quit my job and start a business, brought me into his office, encouraged me, and gave me a Peter Drucker book.

- One of my firm's first clients who told me he saw something in me worth betting on—and I believed him.

- A dear friend and professional colleague who took me to lunch after I sold that first business. She saw that I was spinning after letting go of a big part of my identity. She laughed in my face (literally) and gave me a firm kick in the pants (metaphorically) when I shared that I wasn't sure if I could build a new business as a coach.

- My coaching colleague, who sat across from me at breakfast and created an open, encouraging space that, from out of nowhere, led me to commit to write my first book.

- A book industry colleague, whose passion for helping under-served communities inspired me to use a share of this book's proceeds to establish a scholarship fund for kids in rural areas. It's now up and running.

I could go on and on and on. As I began researching inspiration, stories that were so influential to me came flooding back—like this one: I was twenty-three years old, and starting an internship in Washington at a political consulting firm. This was a plum job that introduced me to some power players in politics, and held the promise of a permanent job after I completed graduate school the following spring. I had cold called dozens of people (this was before email), and networked like crazy to land this unpaid internship. It was my shot. Political jobs are infamously hard to get; most go to kids of political donors, elected officials, or someone who knows someone who is owed a favor.

My first day, I learned that another intern was there that year as well. He was a perfectly nice guy who got the job because his parents knew the firm's head partner. He and that partner would go out at lunch and play tennis at their country club. All of my gravest fears set in. There was one paid job to be awarded at the firm, and it didn't look like I would be getting it. I knew politics was an insider's game, but I began to see that I'd picked the worst profession to make it on merit. I couldn't afford another unpaid internship either, as I had student loans coming due.

The situation was starting to get to me. No matter how hard I worked, I saw no way to overcome my lack of connections. Another one of the partners, one who had grown up similarly to me, took notice. He sat down and asked what was going on. In a moment of total honesty, I told him. He said, "Listen to me. Neither of us grew up like that, and it's okay. You'll be better for it. You can't see it yet, but I promise you. Don't give up."

I remembered those words, and went on to get one of the best first jobs in politics of anyone I knew. I'm sure the partner doesn't remember that ten-minute conversation. But I replayed that tape in my head many times in the years that followed.

These are just a few of the inspiring conversations from my experience. I'll bet you have plenty of your own. When I bring up this concept, the people I'm talking with invariably share inspiring conversations from their lives. I've heard hundreds. No matter who's doing the inspiring, and whether it's for two minutes or two hours, something important is transferred. There's a certain undeniable vibe to them. The exchanges aren't exactly mentorship or advice. In inspiring conversations, nothing is forced. The other person isn't exerting heavy influence on us. It feels more like an invitation to a space into which we can step.

WHAT IS INSPIRATION EXACTLY?

For twenty years, psychology professors Todd Thrash and Andrew Elliot have been studying the process of inspiration. They've produced numerous studies that uncover what transpires within us when we catch the spark of inspirational light.

Thrash and Elliot have determined that inspiration is a culmination of several components coming together, not just a one-sided event. Inspiration may feel as if it just happens, but in fact, there's a rhythm or process to it. Thrash and Elliot have found that inspiration involves three defining elements:[1]

1. **Transcendence:** We can see beyond our ordinary preoccupations or limitations to discover new or better possibilities.
2. **Motivation:** We feel energized, or even compelled, to bring an idea into action or carry it forward.
3. **Evocation:** We are receptive to an influence beyond ourselves that creates the inspiration within us.

We can't will ourselves to be inspired, though we often wish we could. Rather, there's a trigger. This may be a person, an idea, or both. We are exposed to an inspirational force that causes a profound reaction within us. Thrash and Elliot further state that inspiration actually involves two separate component processes: We are inspired *by* something as well as *to* an action. I was inspired *by* a leader *to* go out on my own. It's both an insight and an energetic push.

In an interview with me, Thrash put it this way: "There's always a transmission process of one sort or another. What exactly that transmission means can vary. Transmission could start with an insight, an exemplar, language, or the assistance of another person who helps you envision possibilities you might not have recognized on your own. The person getting inspired has to become aware of a better possibility. That's how the process starts. After that, they get motivated to bring that possibility into fruition."[2]

The research also makes it clear that inspiration can't be forced. It can't feel like manipulation or even influence. In *The Power of Presence*, I wrote about influence. There are many situations where that's the right approach. Inspiration, however, is a different route, though sometimes complementary. Inspiration is an invitation, and since it fosters a personal insight, it can't be heavy handed. A person decides to be inspired for herself, and isn't beholden to someone else's agenda. There's positive energy around it. People don't go home after work and say, "What a great day today, I was influenced!" But they would love to be able to say, "Today I was inspired."

By being an inspirational person, we are not the driver but the catalyst. As Thrash says, "The person who seeks to inspire others would have to look at their task as not making the person inspired, but rather as providing the context where spontaneous processes get triggered."[3]

Think about how much more engaged we would be at work if we were truly inspired in this way—if we had leaders who viewed their jobs as triggers for an inspired workforce. When we're inspired, we work the hardest and most creatively. We don't need to be overmanaged because our energy pulls us along. We elect to do more and go further. It feels a whole lot more like fun than like work.

If we want to have inspired companies, then we need inspirational leaders. And that involves being the kind of leader who communicates in a way that creates the conditions for inspiration in others. It's about making the right connection and letting the inspiration take off from there.

A JOURNEY ALONG THE INSPIRE PATH

After listening to hundreds of stories about inspiring people, it's abundantly clear that the way we trigger inspiration is primarily through conversation. Yes, a book or a song or a poem can inspire us. But people inspire us through interpersonal communication in all of its forms, both verbal and nonverbal. As we've seen, these aren't just any conversations. In my research, certain definitive communications behaviors were present that made the conversations elicitors of inspiration. I've brought these elements together in a model I call the Inspire Path.

Figure I.1 Inspire Path

Inspire Path conversations happen when we communicate in a way that is **present, personal, passionate, and purposeful**. These four factors greatly enhance our inspirational effect. Must all four occur simultaneously? No. Though many inspirational conversations do involve most elements in one form or another.

Further, I call this model a "path" because it's a passage with movement, both for the one inspiring and for the one being inspired. There's no magic formula or predetermined endpoint. It's not a quid pro quo.

Part of being an inspiring person means believing that it's the right way to live, and that it will lead to positive outcomes.

The following pages are organized around the elements of the Inspire Path model, breaking down the behaviors in each section. When we're inspiring, we are:

- **Present:** We're focused on the person in front of us, not distracted by the swirl of our day, visibly stressed, or beholden to our agenda. We keep an open mind and let conversations flow.
- **Personal:** We're authentic and real, and listen generously. We notice what's true about others and help them find their potential.
- **Passionate:** We infuse energy, and manage this as one of our greatest tools. We blend logic and emotion, and show conviction through our presence.
- **Purposeful:** We are intentional. We are willing to serve as role models and engage in courageous discussions about purpose.

If these sound broad to you, you're right. I've written this book in order to define these amorphous concepts at a useful and practical level. Because even though the ideas are simple—e.g., be passionate—the act of showing passion is anything but straightforward. If it were easy, we wouldn't be sitting through so many lifeless meetings led by robotic presenters. As a coach, I make ideas actionable; for years, I've been applying these concepts with my clients. In these pages, I've assembled a guide that combines these concepts with proven actions to help you in your journey to be a more inspiring communicator. It's not the only way. But for my clients, and now hopefully for you, it's an effective way.

You may also find that the ideas presented here go against some of your strongly held beliefs about leadership communications. For example, we've all heard advice about overpreparing for any situation, demonstrating power, remaining unemotional, and keeping a professionally detached demeanor—and we all have preconceived notions about what makes a person effective. Some of these notions are debunked by research, while others are appropriate for some settings but not for others. I ask that you keep an open mind and think back to your own personal experience. This is about inspiring behavior, not directing it.

What was it that inspired you? If you can define it, and direct it outward with clarity, you can inspire others as well.

VALIDATED BY QUANTITATIVE RESEARCH

In developing the Inspire Path model, I listened to hundreds of conversations over the course of five years—from leaders, managers, and teams—and distilled them down to their common themes. I tested the ideas and frameworks with clients to ensure that they worked in practice, and could be replicated by others. I knew before I wrote this book that the tools could significantly increase inspirational effectiveness. But I was still curious about what was most important and valuable in inspiration, and how the behaviors compared to one another.

To that end, I engaged the research firm Harris Poll to conduct original quantitative research to determine what communication behaviors are most inspirational to people.[4] The Harris Poll is one of the most notable and respected surveys in the world, having continuously been in the field of public opinion since 1963. For this research, 2,034 U.S. adults were asked to consider a time when they were inspired by someone whom they've personally known in their adult life and to select the person's inspirational behaviors (in terms of communicating), that had the greatest effect on them. Here are the results:

- The vast majority of U.S. adults (86 percent) report having been inspired by someone that they know personally. This is heartening on a human level!

- Half (50 percent) say the behavior that had the greatest impact was when the person listened to them. This was the most-cited inspirational behavior.
- Forty percent say the greatest impact came from how the person said what they meant and spoke with authenticity.
- Nearly two in five attribute the greatest effect of the inspiring person to:
    - "Giving focused time and attention" (38 percent)
    - "Making the effort to understand where I was coming from" (38 percent)
    - "Showing passion and energy" (38 percent)
    - "Expressing that they saw potential in me" (37 percent)
    - "Helping me see a larger purpose and meaning for myself" (35 percent)

Let's go down a level to provide some meaning behind the numbers. First, for all the emphasis we put on the output of our communications, *listening* has the greatest effect on people. The space we create through listening has power. Second, if all you do is speak authentically and listen well, then you'll be doing a lot as an inspirational communicator. These were the top-two behaviors cited by respondents.

Further, with nearly 40 percent of respondents choosing pretty equally among the rest of the concepts, it's clear that all of these elements are important in inspiration. (Respondents could select as many of the concepts as they wanted.) In fact, only 4 percent said that they were inspired by something else—a good indicator that these are the key behaviors. Again, you don't have to invoke all of these concepts to be inspirational. But the more you do, the greater your opportunity to inspire. You'll see all of these concepts explored throughout the book, in greater detail and with ways to put them into action.

THIS BOOK IS FOR YOU,
IF YOU ARE A LEADER . . . OR WELL, A HUMAN

In the following pages, I'll explore inspiration as a leadership imperative while providing tools and examples primarily in business contexts. Since I work at the intersection of leadership and communications, business provides the tapestry for this book. There are plenty of examples of inspiring conversations in all kinds of business situations, such as:

- Leading change
- Managing people
- Selling an idea or a product
- Communicating a vision
- Dialoguing with the board or investors
- Recruiting and retaining employees
- Growing talent and getting teams to stretch
- Presenting ideas in public speaking settings

You could easily argue that inspiring communications are more important than ever. Factors such as globally dispersed teams, increasingly complex business environments, accelerated change, overwhelmed workforces, and shifting expectations of leaders all create an increasing need for inspiring leadership. The U.S. Army War College introduced a term called VUCA—Volatility, Uncertainty, Complexity, Ambiguity—to define the current state of our world. Certainly this same acronym could be used to describe most business environments.

Tony Bingham has a front-row seat to the skills that companies around the world are prioritizing for their people. The president and CEO of the Association for Talent Development, the world's largest talent development organization, he describes the increasing drumbeat for inspirational leadership this way: "Employees need to believe in the people who are leading them if they're going to stay engaged and give that discretionary effort that unlocks potential, creativity, and innovation. If people don't believe in the people who lead them, they'll find somewhere else to work. Leaders should understand that giving people something to believe in—inspiring them—is more than a platitude or lofty ideal. It's the essence of leadership."[5]

So yes, we need inspirational leadership. But when I talk about leaders, consider it an elastic term. You may be a leader by formal designation or in another kind of way. You may be on a path to leadership, or perhaps you operate as a leader by your very nature. Everything we talk about in this book has an application for executives, managers, young professionals, business owners, community leaders, parents, and pretty much anyone human. Because any one of us can be inspiring at any time, simply by connecting and conversing in inspiring ways.

Further, the way we work, manage, and lead varies greatly among organizations. Many leaders operate as virtual leaders, barely seeing their teams in person at all. Most of the advice in this book can be applied to both in-person and virtual communications. If you add videoconference capabilities to the equation, then all of it can. The ideas also scale. They apply if you're talking to one person across the desk, one thousand across an auditorium, or one million via webcast.

We've begun to see a quiet but steady cultural transformation in the workplace, where being wholehearted, positive, and authentic is appreciated and even expected. In 2013, the University of Pennsylvania's Wharton School management professor Adam Grant wrote a book called *Give and Take*. In it, he argued persuasively and empirically that people who generously give of themselves to help others are the most successful.[6] It was a runaway bestseller. In an interview with me, Grant shared his belief that most people identify with giver values, and if you want more supportive behavior in organizations, the culture needs to just get out of the way: "It's not incentivizing people to be givers, but taking away the disincentives to be givers."[7]

You'll find on these pages many ways to have a positive effect on others. I will even go so far as to guarantee that you'll have a lasting positive impact on people's lives if you put these behaviors into action. But if you want to be truly inspiring, do it because it's the right thing to do. Do it because it starts a virtuous cycle and helps others. Do it because it connects us and strengthens personal fortitude in an otherwise VUCA world. Inspire others because you can.

HOW TO USE THIS BOOK

Here's some good news: there's no lengthy fifteen-step program to follow in these pages. Those kinds of models make me crazy. Instead I wrote the book to be read the way most people work: just-in-time information for use as needed. You can apply as much or as little from these pages as is helpful to you. The chapters can be read in sequence, or you can skip around if there's an area that interests you the most. I've cross-referenced throughout, so you can jump around easily for deeper dives into the content.

I also wrote the book the way adult learners think—through contemplation, discussion, and then application of an idea. In each chapter, I discuss research and examples from a few angles to explore the concept, and then end with a "concept in action" section that shows how to put the ideas into your daily life. It's worthwhile to reflect and cogitate, but in the end, nothing happens unless we get to action. You'll also find a leader's guide in the appendix to prep for conversations or to stay on track.

Finally, I use many stories and examples throughout the book—often about leaders I've worked with and seen in action. Due to the privacy of coaching, all client stories are composites of various clients over the years. Identifying information has been changed while preserving the educational aspects of the examples. Even in diverse situations, coaching issues are remarkably similar at heart. I've always found it reassuring how much we all have in common.

I hope that you find, as I have in this process, how much of an impact we have by doing a few things with intention and meaning. You have everything you need to be an inspiring communicator—a leader who creates energetic engagement and enduring followership; a manager who fosters excitement and excellence; a colleague who builds potential and possibilities in others; a person who lights up a room.

Here's the path.

PART

I

PRESENT

THE GIFT
OF ATTENTION

CHAPTER 1

ARE YOU TALKING TO ME?

"She was there for me."

"He made the time."

"Her door was always open."

"He invested in me."

When I've asked people to describe someone who inspired them, one of the first comments is that the person was noticeably present. People who inspire us are both physically and mentally available to us. They focus on us. They give us the gift of their time, and just as important, the gift of their attention.

That attention affects us in a multitude of ways.

How we focus our attention reveals what we care about—whether or not we mean it to. On a basic human level, we crave positive attention from those who matter to us. We're social animals. Isolation hurts us. It's hard to overestimate the very human need to have others bear witness to what's happening in our lives.

Certainly the connections we feel form the fabric of our days and influence our attitudes. Gallup's well-cited research on what makes productive workgroups shows that those who say they have a best friend at work are significantly more likely to strive for quality and to get recognition and encouragement.[1]

Leaders should also keep in mind that their attention casts a large shadow and has an inflated impact. Psychologists have long studied how power shapes attention. Susan Fiske, professor of psychology and public affairs at Princeton University, has found that that we pay more attention to those above us in social hierarchies.[2] Dacher Keltner, professor of psychology at Berkeley, has published numerous studies showing that being in power makes us not just pay less attention to others, but to actually *feel* less for them.[3]

This power differential is important. Think about it. When you're a leader, people are watching you closely. They notice how you enter a room and where you sit as well as your tone of voice and demeanor. However, you're more prone to overlook the people at the levels below you. You are less likely to be tuned in to them, perhaps lost in your own concerns, while you're being studied intently. Many leaders don't realize that this phenomenon is happening, or they ignore it, or they let it wear them down. This explains the considerable misunderstandings and frustrations often seen in hierarchical relationships.

When you're a leader, people are watching you more closely and you're more prone to overlook them.

For leaders, presence is a blinking red light that signifies importance. Being fully present at key times has a motivational impact. When a leader actually pays real attention to us, it feels great. We feel special. The capacity to inspire is heightened.

BEING PRESENT
CHANGES THE CONVERSATION

At a theoretical level, the conversations we have may seem pretty similar. If we're present enough for a dialogue, then we're accomplishing what we need. But if we're truly present, that's when the shift happens.

In workshops, I lead an exercise to show the impact of focused attention. (I'll share here so you can experience it vicariously.) The setup is easy. Working in pairs, participants discuss recent weekend plans—with a twist. In the first round, I have the speakers talk about their plans, and instruct the listeners to act as if they don't actually care all that much about what the speakers are sharing. They can check their phones, look around the room, and practice spotty eye contact—whatever is in the realm of normal, disengaged behavior.

The energy in the room during Round 1 is low-key. Participants share conversations like this:

What did you do this weekend?

Saw a movie.

Oh yeah, what did you see?

The new Bourne movie. It was pretty good, but I thought the last one was better.

I'm not big on action movies, but I do like the Bourne series. I haven't seen a movie in a while though. Just seems like we never get to it.

I know what you mean. The weekend goes so fast.

You know the drill; it's your typical catch up. Short conversations that lose steam quickly, with people looking to me for the "all clear" to stop talking as the exchange devolves into uncomfortably lowered gazes.

Then we go to Round 2. This time, the listeners are encouraged to be completely present to their discussion partners. They are asked to orient their posture toward each other, make sustained eye contact, and tune out distractions. Listeners are told to be curious, to notice the reactions of the other person, and to ask questions about what the speaker seems to have energy around. Otherwise, they have the exact same conversation.

Except they don't. This time the discussion is completely different. There's a high level of energy in the room. People are laughing, gesturing, and listening intently. They are mirroring each other's body language. I can barely get the participants to stop talking.

And time after time, when we debrief, I hear that the act of paying attention changes the conversation significantly. In Round 1, the speaker could barely discuss the most basic of experiences without a present listener. The conversation is superficial and brief. In Round 2, the experience is markedly changed, looking more like this:

What did you do this weekend?

Saw a movie.

I noticed you smiled when you said that. What brought that on?

You caught that! Yes, I was thinking about my son's reaction. I took him to see the Bourne movie, which was the first grown-up movie he's seen with me. It felt like a rite of passage . . . something I used to do with my dad. We loved to see action flicks together.

I can tell that spending time with your son is really important to you. What else do you like to do?

We're both into hockey, and love going to games. We don't go very often though; that's harder to plan, especially with my travel schedule. Now that I think about it, it's not about the content of what we do, but the time we spend together that makes it memorable. Even a quick trip to the movies was meaningful. I'm going to think of activities we can do on the spot, like . . .

If you were a fly on the wall in the room, you would think you were looking at a group of old friends catching up, or colleagues hashing out a serious topic. You'd find it hard to believe it's the same people who could barely keep a conversation going! While weekend plans may have initiated both conversations, in Round 2, a present listener enabled the speaker to expand the topic, often in surprising ways. The speaker covered more ground, the conversation ventured into areas of meaning and importance, and both the speaker and the listener learned more about each other.

When I conduct this exercise with intact work groups, participants say they learned more about their colleagues in the five-minute exchange than in all the years they've known them. I've heard people say they discovered something new about themselves simply by having a curious listener. And just about everyone admits that the contrast between the conversations is remarkable.

By sitting in front of someone and investing fully, we create an inspirational space. Not so difficult, or so it seems. While it's fairly straightforward to be a present communicator, it's hard to find one. If we can make the commitment, especially in relationships where we want to inspire, we can make an impact by essentially doing nothing but choosing to pay earnest attention.

This same effect comes into play in a large group or public setting. Ever meet someone at a networking event who actually took the time to get to know you? That person stands out. And I'm pretty sure you've been to a networking event where someone looked over your shoulder to see who else was in the room, and can recall how diminishing that feels. (No wonder so many people consider networking to be a distasteful, or even a little soul-crushing, chore.)

Our presence is an invitation to inspiration. It's the lead-in, the door opener, the hook. Yet, how easy it is to squander this opportunity to use our focused attention to make an impact. I was once brought in to work with a senior leader, Sam, who needed to unite a team behind a new and bold vision. She asked me to attend her all-hands meeting, where her entire team had gathered from around the globe. Sam, who had grown up at the company but had spent most of her time in a different product division, was an unknown quantity to her current team. This meeting was Sam's chance to introduce her vision and rally the troops around it.

Expectations were high. Everyone milled about, buzzing with eagerness to hear what was in store. As the start time neared and passed, you could see people glancing at their watches. Excitement lapsed into concern, and then into annoyance. Finally, Sam walked into the room fifteen minutes late, finishing a call, and took the stage hurriedly. She began her comments by telling everyone that she'd been managing a crisis so would be talking off the cuff. She was there, but everyone in that room knew she wasn't present. There was zero inspiration happening that day. In fact, Sam created an inspiration deficit.

Sam's team needed to be optimistic and engaged to accomplish its mission. After that meeting, I overheard several people lamenting the fact that the company had picked the wrong person to lead the cause.

LET'S GET REAL: TIME IS MONEY

You may be thinking that you'd love to be fully present, but it sounds like it takes more time than you have to give. Many of us feel as though we can barely get through our inbox by the end of the day. Which leads to what gets in the way of being fully present: We're distracted and busy. Yet, some people manage to be fully present to what matters to them. They have equally demanding jobs and the same twenty-four hours to play with each day. So, how much of our distracted attention is our own doing?

Social researchers would argue, *a lot*.

How much of our distracted attention results from our own choices? More than we'd like to admit.

We've concocted the perfect storm of divided attention. In a very short time, we've become a society that communicates in short bursts, and largely via intermediaries. The Internet, mobile phones, and other portable electronics make it far easier to talk *through* something rather than *with* someone. And we can't stop ourselves.

Research indicates that we spend about eight hours online every day, and send or receive an average of 400 text messages each month.[4] Internet addiction is such a heated topic that it came close to being included in the *Diagnostic and Statistical Manual of Mental Disorders* (DSM), the standard guide used to classify mental disorders in the United States. (Internet gaming addiction did make it in, by the way.)

In the space of a decade and a half, we've gone from using technology as needed to never being away from our phones without feeling a sense of serious unease. A 2015 study found that 71 percent of us sleep beside our phones, and 3 percent sleep with them in our hands. We go to our phones first thing, with 35 percent of us grabbing them ahead of our coffee or toothbrushes. Nearly half of us say we wouldn't make it a day without our smartphones.[5]

The way we talk to each other has fundamentally changed. We don't have time to be present because we're present to technology. It's become a rarity in modern business (or life) to have a simple conversation without competition from other sources. It's become socially accepted to glance at our emails during a conversation, or even to read our phones in a group setting or meeting. Imagine picking up a magazine and reading it in the middle of a meeting at work! That would be seen as an affront to others, and socially obtuse. We pretend that we need to be "on call" though it's widely understood that this rationale is bent constantly.

Recently, I was asked to observe one of my clients in a board meeting. I sat toward the back of the boardroom where I could see the screens of the board members. While the CEO was talking, I watched the board members reading their email, scanning news articles, and even looking at Facebook. This from the people who have a personal, fiduciary responsibility to the company! The average weekly team status meeting is in deep trouble.

Conference calls, the typical way most companies communicate, fare even worse. I've been asked to conduct entire sessions on how to command attention in a virtual setting when participants are clearly multitasking. We've come to expect the clicking keyboard when participants forget to hit mute, or the pregnant pause when someone addresses a question to a participant who isn't paying attention. This has become such a norm that even when videoconferencing is an option—which has been shown to significantly increase engagement—people elect to not be on camera so they can more easily multitask.

One positive sign is that people and businesses are beginning to realize that we're missing important parts of the interpersonal dynamic. In 2015, a Pew Research study of mobile behaviors and attitudes found that 89 percent of cell phone owners said they used their phones during their last gathering, and 82 percent felt it hurt the conversation.[6]

So we check our phones, send text messages, glance at our email, or scan social media while real people are right in front of us. But at least we acknowledge that there's a price.

THE PRICE OF DISTRACTION

Virginia Tech researchers sought to determine what actually happens to conversations when mobile phones are introduced. They found that even when a phone isn't making a noise and is only in eyesight, conversations are diminished. The *mere presence* of the phone sitting on the table draws attention away from the conversation. Our attention is subtly drawn outward and away from the other person; we can miss facial expressions, tone, and other cues that have significant meaning.

Even when a phone is in sight, sitting silently, our conversation is diminished.

The study concluded that conversations without a mobile phone in sight were seen as superior and included higher levels of empathy. This finding was consistent across age, gender, ethnicity, and mood.[7]

Sherry Turkle, MIT professor and founder of MIT's Initiative on Technology and Self, has been one of the most active and vocal researchers in this area. An early voice in the digital culture conversation, Turkle was heralded in the 1990s as an advocate who truly understood technology's potential. In her two most recent books, *Alone Together* and *Reclaiming Conversation*, Turkle asserts that technology is harming our ability to have meaningful, face-to-face conversations. What's at stake isn't just how we talk, but how we understand one another as humans.

Turkle's research explores how people spend more time connected to one another electronically, yet say they are lonelier, more emotionally disconnected, and anxious. Online, we present a sanitized, curated, edited version of ourselves through email, text messages, and social media. People can choose to be focused elsewhere any time they like, and opt-out of the most important events in their lives, especially difficult moments. Turkle discusses how it's even common to see people on their phones at funerals.[8]

In her widely watched Ted.com talk, Turkle warns of the "Goldilocks effect," where we have begun to prefer a safe distance from others: "not too close, not too far, just right."[9] Her research shows our dependence on technology is degrading our ability to empathize, supporting the Virginia Tech study's hypothesis. We take ourselves out of difficult conversations—or any conversation—by diverting our attention. We fail to notice what needs to be seen.

We take ourselves out of any hard conversation by diverting our attention.

Turkle insists that we need to be present during the not-so-fun moments to show our humanity. These moments uncover who we really are and what matters to us. "Most important," says Turkle, "we all really need to listen to each other, including the boring bits. Because it's when we stumble or hesitate or lose our words that we reveal ourselves to each other."

Inspire Path conversations are about, and happen within, these human moments. They require our full attention so we don't miss any of the dynamics in front of us—especially the real, messy, or uncomfortable parts.

It's said that people have three core needs: to be seen, heard, and understood. Just in the act of being fully present, we are knocking off the first two. You can go a long way to being inspiring to another person just by showing up and being in the moment. By having a focused, real conversation, you are already standing out from the typical distracted half-conversations that make up the majority of our daily communications. And by being willing to hear the words and tone—and to see the other person's nonverbal behavior—you open the door to deep, human connection.

CONCEPT IN ACTION

BEING PRESENT:
A PRETTY AMAZING PRESENT

So we know that we need to be present to have conversations that count. Listening is instrumental to inspiring, and certainly we can't listen if we're distracted and don't even catch what the other person is saying. But how can we be more present in the daily rush of living and working? I said before that it's straightforward. We do it all the time when the stakes are high and we care the most. What's hard is prioritizing being present when life has other plans. Here I am writing about this concept in a book; I've studied all the research behind the benefit of presence to our relationships, and I coach CEOs and large corporations on the concept. Still, I'm the first to acknowledge that I struggle with it. The first step in making progress may be admitting that we need more than a desire to be present. We need a plan.

For most people it's unrealistic to resolve to be present for every interaction. Much of our day is about getting things done. There are, however, certain conversations where we do want to connect and inspire another person to expand perspective or take action. Conversations where we want to be all-in. Conversations that matter.

When you're having those conversations, there are a number of ways to show how important the conversation (and therefore, the person) is to you:

Create a distraction-free zone

Willpower is wonderful, but most of us don't have as much of it as we need. It's far easier to put ourselves in a place where we can't be distracted than to resist distractions by our computers, our phones, or by office interruptions.

If you want to have an Inspire Path conversation, create a zone where you can't help but focus on the other person. If you're in your office, power down your computer and put your phones on do not disturb. Physically move away from your desk, and sit at a table or go to a conference room without taking your electronics. Or get out of your office entirely; move the conversation to lunch or a coffee. (But don't put your phone on the table, even if it's turned off.) If on a conference call, let the other person know that you're shutting down email and other distractions, and request the same consideration.

When you show how seriously you're taking a conversation, it raises the importance for everyone else as well.

When you show how seriously you're taking a conversation, it raises the importance for everyone else as well.

Use the power of pause

How frequently we rush from one meeting to another, without stopping to consider each as its own specific connection point, with a unique set of goals and expectations. At the end of the day, it's a muddled mess of interactions and can be hard to detangle one from the other.

To be present, learn the power of pause. Take a few moments before the conversation and sit quietly. Take a few deep breaths to get oxygen to your brain, shake off stress, and center your energy. Reflect on what you want to get out of the dialogue. What action do you want to inspire? What feeling do you want to create?

In Chapter 2, I discuss the concept of a situational intention, a crucial pause before important conversations to determine "how do I want people to feel as a result of this exchange?" Situational intention requires the speaker to dig into the feelings that she is trying to evoke in the other party. After all, we process in emotional terms. If you want someone to feel excited then you need to project excitement.

By using this pause to consider what feeling you want to create, you reorient your brain away from the external noise or internal concerns, and toward the moment in front of you.

Get curious

Our conversations are designed in our heads, and then presented to others. In this way, many times we predetermine or shape the content before the conversation has actually begun. In any conversation, there are four players: the two people talking, and the two inner voices of the people talking. (Much more about this dynamic in Chapter 6.) We can pay more attention to our own inner voice, which is feeding us our message points, trying to redirect to our chosen topic, assessing how it's going, and angling to make us look smart or funny. But if we're listening to our own internal dialogue, then we're not being present to the other person.

An easy fix: Get curious. Look to see what the other person is interested in and ask questions about it. Don't assume you know the answers. Let your mind go with the conversation.

Hold the space

Sherry Turkle talks about how we need to preserve "sacred spaces" of undivided attention around times that matter to us. We can also do this around *conversations* that matter to us. When we hold the space for other people, free of distraction, with full attention, then we provide the opportunity for them to process their own thoughts through dialogue. Make no mistake: this is an important and inspiring gesture of connection that people rarely get. In fact, we pay psychologists and coaches handsomely to offer this service.

By holding the space, you don't rush the conversation either explicitly or implicitly. You designate a time for it, and you honor it. You don't interrupt or direct the conversation. Rather, you let it unfold. Many of our best insights happen when another person creates the space for us to truly think.

Many of our best insights happen when another person creates the space for us to truly think.

Say that it's important

We all fall prey to the *transparency illusion*, which is a psychological phenomenon stating that we overestimate how well others can guess what we're thinking.[10] We're actually pretty awful at knowing the motivation of others. We fill in the blanks and create reasons for others' behavior in the absence of solid information. We're not even very good at understanding the motives of people we live with, so you can imagine how bad we are with colleagues at work!

It can benefit the conversation to state our motivations at the outset so there's no guessing required. If we're trying to make ourselves be present because the conversation is important, then let the other person know that. It's fine to come out and say something such as:

- "This is important to me so I want to fully focus on your issue for the next hour."
- "My goal with this discussion is to help you see what's possible for yourself."
- "Nothing else is as much of a priority right now as this conversation."

There are countless ways to say that the conversation matters. Put it in your words, and put it out there.

Show receptive body language

Our body language sends subtle and not-so-subtle signals about what we're willing to receive from the other party. Body language has meaning (which is an important reason to use videoconferencing for meetings if it's an option). As the workshop exercise about weekend schedules showed, when people don't see you as receptive, they limit their communications. We'll discuss body language and its meaning in depth in Chapter 9. For now, just consider a few critical components of your nonverbal communication.

Orientation: As much as possible, orient yourself so you're facing the other person. Try to get your shoulders square with that person, as if you are speaking from your chest. If it's a group discussion, alternate having your torso face different people in the room. Keep your arms and legs uncrossed; you don't want to appear to be closed off. Step around physical separators such as desks and lecterns.

Eyes: When we want to know someone's intent, we look into his eyes. If he averts his eyes, we assume negative intent such as untrustworthiness or disinterest. Make sustained eye contact, and keep it on people, not things. It's okay to look away while you're thinking, but then come back to the other person. Keep your eyes soft, which shows receptiveness. Soft eyes are relaxed at the corners, not focused intently like we're reading small print in a book. To practice soft eyes, look straight ahead and focus lightly, while still preserving your peripheral vision.

Smile: While there are other ways to show warmth and approachability, smiling is the most universal. All too often our inner thoughts show up on our face without our even knowing. Perhaps you've had the experience of someone asking you what's wrong when you didn't think anything was! Many people have faces that, when relaxed, turn downward in a frown. (I'm one of them.) All this is to say: Smile early and smile often.

CHOOSE THE CONVERSATION
IN FRONT OF YOU

An Inspire Path conversation requires you to be completely *in* the conversation. We have more distractions and diversions for our attention than at any time in human history. We face enormous choices to entertain us and connect us with the world. Yet, we're lonelier and less connected than ever. We have pressures on our attention and work expectations that have bled over into a 24/7 workday. And yet, we limit our own bandwidth by the choices we make. But the truth is, we have a choice in how we spend our time.

Whether you're reading this to inspire one person, or to build followership for an entire company, choose to give the gift of being present to the conversations you're in. There's no better place to start.

TAKEAWAYS

FROM CHAPTER 1

- To inspire people, you first need to give them your focus and attention. It's how they know you're invested in them.

- When we give another person our full attention versus our divided attention, the conversation changes.

- We communicate primarily through intermediaries—email, text messages, social media—in which we've traded efficiency for true connection. Social psychologists have found that we're losing the ability to empathize due to overuse of technology.

- Norms are quickly developing and changing around what is socially acceptable in terms of technology usage, and its impact. Recent research shows that while most people use technology in interpersonal situations, they also believe it hurts the conversation.

- To be fully present to the conversation, eliminate distractions, use a reflective pause, get curious, hold a space, say it's important, and show receptive body language.

CHAPTER 2

THE STORIES WE TELL OURSELVES WHILE WE'RE FALLING APART

2014 was a weird year.

Let me set the stage: My first book came out at the tail end of 2011, and I'd spent 2012 and part of 2013 doing the author marketing that goes along with publishing a book these days. It was busy but manageable. I continued to work with my core client base in Washington, and manage the activity of being a business owner, leadership coach, and a working parent.

Then, like a switch, everything changed. My book hit an inflection point, and I began getting all kinds of new and exciting work opportunities. Companies around the world were inviting me to speak or to coach their leaders. I was asked to do programs connected to Harvard, Duke, and Georgetown, and to lead global workshops. Media brands I'd admired my entire life asked me to write for them. When people find so much meaning in a book that they want to bring it into their organizations, that's just about the most affirming thing that can happen to an author. This all felt amazing . . . in the beginning.

My mother noticed first (as mothers do). "You look worn down," she said. I ignored her, confident that all this wonderful and rewarding work couldn't possibly be a negative. After all, I wanted to do it! I'd worked hard for this. I'd begun to spend more time on planes, so much so that when I'd get together with colleagues we'd spend most of our time trading frequent flyer tips. I was getting sick more frequently (especially after a particularly important trip), and developed acid reflux. At one point, I caught such a bad eye infection that my eye was halfway swollen shut. (Apologies to the participants in that workshop. I know it was ugly.)

Finally, I woke up one morning with a cracked molar from grinding my teeth, requiring significant and painful dental work over the course of months. It was a literal breaking point. Something was out of whack, and it appeared to be me.

That summer I decided to take a step back and reassess my workload, choices, and just about everything else. The thing is, I never felt that my work suffered. Especially for the times that really mattered, no matter my stress level, I felt that I showed up prepared, professional, and on point. But here's where it's handy to be a coach and have lots of coaching friends to talk with. I dug deeper.

The story I kept telling myself was that this work was something I had to do—because after all, I'd asked for it. I'd worked to be where I was. And it was interesting to me. I'd be crazy not to do every bit of the work! I also kept a refrain in my head that this pace was somehow temporary, and that no one noticed the wear and tear but my closest friends and family. It affected nothing else.

That's right, I had bought into my own stories, even though I spend so much of my time coaching other leaders not to fall into the trap of believing theirs. That's how powerful the pull of our own perception bias can be. We'll do a whole lot of searching to find evidence to confirm what we already think.

This story ends on a good note. Through reflection, trial and error, and nail-biter decisions, I did finally get myself to a place where I could see everything as a choice, with a series of trade-offs. I figured out what kind of work I wanted to be doing more of, and made it a priority. I delegated work that I personally enjoyed, but that no longer fit in the larger picture. (This was hard.) I put parameters around my travel, even if it sometimes meant saying no to compelling or lucrative work. (This was even harder.) I prioritized my family and health, and reset my definition of business success. By the end of 2014, I was in one of the most content and fulfilled periods of my life. Thankfully, while I'm writing this in 2016, I'm still here.

OVERWHELM: TOO MUCH OF SOMETHING WE NEVER WANTED

I'm well aware of the irony that a coach who helps others deal with overwhelm is starting this chapter with her own story of, ahem, overwhelm. I chose to be upfront about it because it brings the issue into the light. I believe that overwhelm is one of the most pressing issues in our companies—and in our larger society. Overwhelm often doesn't look like people spinning out of control, but is a grinding pressure in those who appear to be holding everything together.

Overwhelm often doesn't look like someone spinning out of control, but is a grinding pressure in those who appear to be holding everything together.

In 2014, two of my colleagues—*Washington Post* reporter Brigid Schulte and leadership coach Scott Eblin—tackled overwhelm in their well-acclaimed books: Schulte's *Overwhelmed* and Eblin's *Overworked and Overwhelmed*. Their research added to a growing number of voices raising the red flag on the unsustainability of the way so many people live and work. In an interview with me, Eblin described his surprise at the intensity of the drumbeat for people to find ways out of their own overwhelm.

Eblin has been conducting leadership workshops for years, but he found that the desire to find a sustainable pace trumps all. He concludes that people can't focus on any kind of professional development until they feel in control of themselves: "The conclusion I've come to is that people may be hungry for information or tactics they can use to improve their leadership. But they are thirsty for strategies to be present and self-manage. People die of thirst first. You can go longer without food than water."[1]

I see a wide range of leaders in my work. From our first meeting, I can detect whether their energy is in a state of overwhelm or in a calm, centered, and focused mode. Regardless of the demands of the position, or what's happening right outside their office doors, some leaders maintain an oasis of calm. Others exist somewhere between a low-level hum and outright state of panic, depending on the day. I don't have special powers—we all have that ability to intuit the energetic field of others. (For more on the science of mood contagion, see Chapter 7.) This matters greatly for our challenge of being inspiring and connected.

We intuit the energetic field of others.

Let's say you have a meeting with a leader in your organization. She comes in late looking distracted and harried. Her stress is palpable over some fire just put out. Then she proceeds to run the meeting in a way that shows she needs to get out quickly and deal with something else more important.

How inspiring will this leader be? Not very, if at all.

When we are around people who seem overwhelmed, our primary instinct is to distance ourselves from them. We have a self-protective mechanism in place to prevent any contagion in our own psychic worlds. We disconnect.

If we're the ones who are overwhelmed, we can't have an Inspire Path conversation when our audience would prefer to get away from us.

Now consider how much of this frenetic energy is exhibited in our organizations every single day. In some cultures, it's the norm. In others, it's even a badge of honor. I've worked with entrepreneurs who absolutely believe that stress and overwhelm is their "edge" to stay at the top of their game. They fail to see how their own presence produces chronic stress in the people around them. (Yet, they'll typically seek coaching to alleviate some of their own stressful side effects like an inability to keep innovating or to maintain work/life balance.)

Research shows that chronic, long-term stress and overwhelm take an enormous toll on us physically and mentally. They alter our brain chemistry to keep us in constant fight or flight mode, causing our amygdala to flood our bodies with stress hormones. Stress has been linked to high blood pressure, digestive issues, sleep disturbances, anxiety, headaches, anger, chest pains, strokes, and substance abuse.[2] This is something most of us not only know, but have at some point experienced firsthand.

Like a narrowing lens, overwhelm takes away our ability to see the full extent of what's in front of us. It limits creativity, agility, and ideation. It overrides empathy. The more information we have running through our heads, the worse our decisions get. When our brains reach a point of overload, we take shortcuts. For example, instead of examining the full range of quality information available, we'll rely on recent data.[3] We can feel like a whipped flag in the wind, reacting to what's in front of us without stepping back to be proactive or strategic.

Overwhelm limits creativity, agility, and ideation, and overrides empathy.

One culprit—or enabler—of overwhelm is perfectionism. As I mentioned earlier in this chapter, those who are susceptible to overwhelm are often high-functioning individuals trying to tackle it all. I say this from a personal place as well, as a recovering perfectionist. Perfectionists can get a lot done, and we hold ourselves to a high bar. We are even proud of our high standard for ourselves, even when it's killing us.

A few months ago, I ran across a quote from author Elizabeth Gilbert that hit me square in the face. She said that perfectionism was the "haute couture high-end version of fear." Perfectionism, she explained, is a way of trying to put up an impervious front due to our fear of failing, being inadequate, or not measuring up. It may be a socially acceptable form of fear, but it's fear. "Perfectionism," she quipped, "is just fear in really good shoes."[4]

Whether feeling uncertainty, padding our experience, or berating ourselves for something that hasn't lived up to our expectations, there's a common driver—and it's not pretty. Author and lecturer Marianne Williamson posits that there are actually two motivating forces behind our behavior: love and fear.[5] Any other emotions we have are subcategories of these two. In the workplace, love can mean passion for our work, care for our teams, enjoyment for making a difference, or deep satisfaction. Fear may mean worry about being successful, insecurity about not measuring up, mentally checking out, or engaging in undermining behavior to secure our status. All of the good and bad behavior we see in organizations can be segmented into these dichotomies. Consider how these emotions line up:

LOVE IS . . .	FEAR IS . . .
Generosity	Insecurity
Confidence	Stress
Openness	Perfectionism
Receptiveness	Negativity
Positivity	Territorialism
Gratitude	Judgment
Passion	Jealousy
Creativity	Withdrawal
Acceptance	One-upmanship
Support	Guilt
Abundance	Scarcity
Joy	Dejection

I'll admit the first time I heard this concept I thought it sounded too pat, and more than a little woo-woo for a business setting. But I see this play out with increasing clarity the more I've experienced in organizations in my career and in my coaching work. The VP who is acting territorially around a major initiative? Fear. The CEO who inspires everyone with her passion to change health care? Love. The consulting partner who can't delegate? Fear. The change agent who is willing to risk his personal reputation to move the organization to a better place? Love.

We operate from a place of fear more often than we realize. When we do, we aren't inspiring or connecting. We're pushing people away. And most of the time we don't even realize it because we're merely surviving in overwhelm mode. Fear-based behavior is reactive and sometimes even irrational. This is why it can be so hard to reason with someone in this state.

I once coached a CEO who was trying to lead a major change initiative for his company. He was exceedingly bright, gregarious, and caring. By the time he called me for coaching, he was also burned out, frustrated, and irritated by his team's apparent inability to change. In talking with his team, I learned that even though he was well-liked, he was also seen as micromanaging and unpredictable. He was afraid to let the smallest details go, causing the team to feel underused and untrusted. His closest colleagues expressed concern about his capacity and the stress they saw in him. Instead of feeling positive and inspired by the change which was his goal, the organization reflected back what others saw in him: stress and concern.

We may think we're hiding our overwhelm, but it leaks out.

For people to change, they need to take a risk. Taking a risk requires confidence, hope, and positivity. How many leaders are just like my client, expecting others to soar into the unknown while they themselves are showing fear? In my experience, most change initiatives fail in part because leaders don't make the change look like something others would want to undertake.

It's not just change leaders who do this; it's all of us who want to show up in an inspiring way while we feel underwater. Whether it's me during 2014 or you right now, stress and overload absolutely change the way others feel about being around us. Even when we think we're good at hiding it—it leaks out. It's far better to address it at the source.

CONCEPT IN ACTION

YES, I'M OVERWHELMED. WHERE'S MY LIFELINE?

To be present, physically and mentally, we can't be so wound up in our own frenzy. For many of us, overwhelm may come and go. It can be hard to get a handle on.

The first step to addressing overwhelm is realizing that you're in it. Some people experience physical symptoms of stress or feel mentally whipped, and it's apparent. Others hide behind the illusion that they can somehow put more hours in the day, or survive on less sleep than anyone else. But deep down, if we create time for reflection, we actually do know. Ask yourself a few key questions:

- Am I, more often than not, feeling the emotions in the fear column?
- When I think about the day ahead, does it fill me with excitement or feel burdensome?
- What priorities for myself are unmet on a regular basis?
- How often do I feel on top of things?

Once we begin to notice that we've gone into overdrive we can begin to develop strategies for how to get ourselves back to a place where we can be present—and in a better place to connect with others. Too often we slip into overwhelm unwittingly and don't realize it until we're underwater. Instead, it's more helpful to recognize impending stress and to plan for a workaround. Contemplate this: Your schedule, your workload, or your office demands are what they are. They are a neutral variable, with no emotional charge. It's your reaction to them that causes you stress. Another person could react to the same situation very differently. Your stressful schedule could cause someone else boredom or indifference. You create your reaction. This means that you have the ultimate control and choice in the matter. People get themselves out of the hole of overwhelm all the time. It may not be easy, but it's possible. I see it happen routinely and watch lives change. How do they do it? By challenging their assumptions, pausing to hit reset, and using strategic intention to move forward.

We can't change anything unless we accept it first.

CHALLENGE YOUR ASSUMPTIONS

Viktor Frankl, noted psychiatrist, author, and concentration camp survivor, wrote in his heartbreakingly beautiful memoir, *Man's Search for Meaning*: "Between stimulus and response there is a space. In that space is our power to choose our response. In our response lies our growth and our freedom."[6] Overwhelm hits us so fast that it feels like one solid event. But it's not. Overwhelm is only the response. Something else is the stimulus. If we want to have less overwhelm then we need to understand what the trigger is that's causing our reaction, and be able to take advantage of that space, or pause, to change our reaction.

Normally, when we have a stress trigger, we go straight into reaction mode. There's almost an underlying assumption that X leads to Y. *My boss yelled at me in a meeting so I'm going to get upset. My board presentation is today so I'm going to be on edge.* These stress triggers create negative spirals that undermine our confidence. Once the cycle starts it knocks us off our game.

Our bodies are willing accomplices. When we feel a threat, our brain responds. Our blood leaves the pre-frontal cortex, or the thinking part of our brains, and goes into the amygdala, the reptilian, reactive part of our brain that regulates emotions. Just as if there were a tiger chasing us, our bodies react with increased blood pressure, stress hormones, and other physiological symptoms. We also have a hard time coming back to a calm state. We all have stress triggers, though we experience them uniquely and with varying intensity.

But as Frankl so eloquently notes, we are overlooking a space between the action and our reaction. In that space we have the capacity to change the outcome. We have the ability to choose our response. *My boss yelled at me and I'll decide how to react. My board presentation is today so I'll choose to do a few things to stay light and relaxed.* We simply have to recognize our stressor, acknowledge its impact in the moment, and pause. We have to be ready to take a different approach, to adapt a new perspective, to employ a new narrative.

In the 1970s, organizational scholar and Harvard professor Chris Argyris, along with his MIT colleague Donald Schön, introduced the concept of double loop learning.[7] Since then, other derivative organizational theories have followed—the work still pivotal in organizational and personal change models.

To simplify the idea, it's essentially this:

$$\text{Assumptions} \rightarrow \text{Actions} \rightarrow \text{Results}$$

Argyris and Schön argued that when people want to change the results that they're getting, they typically try different actions. They may go through this "single loop" over and over again with lackluster or incremental results. However, for significant change to take place, people need to question their underlying assumptions, thoughts, and values. This "double loop learning" makes possible a host of entirely new actions to effect sustained change.

Let's take this out of theory and into practice, using a common work scenario. Say you want to be promoted (the result) which requires you to raise your visibility (your assumption). So you go about taking actions to do that: attending more after-work events, asking people to lunch, and requesting to be included in high-profile meetings. You could stay in this loop for a very long time, coming up with new and different ways to increase your exposure before finally exhausting yourself. You will make incremental progress, absolutely. At the end of the period many more people will know your name. Yet, you're no closer to getting that promotion.

Now, let's look at what possibilities would open up if you took a strategic pause, went back, and challenged your assumption that raising your visibility would lead to promotion. First, you might do some research, and gain some behind-the-scenes data on how the last several people at your level were promoted. What did they do? What alliances did they have? What qualifications did they bring? What leadership qualities did they demonstrate? Suppose you were to learn that a handful of powerful influencers were vocal advocates for every person who'd been promoted. While broad visibility was a factor, a larger factor seemed to be a few close-knit relationships with select people who could sway opinion. Now the actions you might choose to take would look quite different—and include ones you *couldn't even see* before questioning your assumption. Instead of spending hours networking broadly, you might instead invest time trying to get on projects and attend events with one or two opinion leaders so that those individuals can get to know you better. You might put your energy into relationship building with a select group—taking a surgical approach. When you change your assumption, you expand your repertoire of available actions and increase your capacity for results.

Now let's use a real example based on more general assumptions, a little less cut and dried with some messy reality thrown in. A client of mine—we'll call her Rebecca—is a highly effective leader and a high-potential being groomed for a C-level job at her company. Once a quarter, she's called to present to the board, and that's where she's run into serious issues. Even though she speaks to groups constantly as part of her job, it's a whole different animal with the board. She gets very nervous, overly scripts herself, and worries about not knowing answers to these brusque and whip-smart board member's questions. Before I worked with her, she'd spent a year trying different actions to perform better in board meetings. She increased her preparation, brought additional data to meetings, and moved the order of her presentation on the schedule. Yet, the board's feedback wasn't improving. In fact, they were voicing concern about her future potential at the company.

When we started working together, we began by working through her assumptions: What did she think made for a good board presentation? What was her value to the board? What was she in that room to do? Through this process she discovered that her assumption was that she needed to project a perfect image, never miss a beat, and have a quick response to every question posed. After further reflection and observing colleagues who managed well at the board level, she realized that what really brought value was to express an informed point of view, be flexible in her discussion, and facilitate key points rather than sticking to a tight script.

This realization was incredibly freeing to Rebecca on one hand, but scary as hell on the other. Even though she got it intellectually, not clinging to her old way of preparing seemed like a major risk. So we started small, with meetings that weren't with the board. She practiced preparing less detailed content, spending more time getting her head around her high-level thoughts and speaking off-the-cuff. Afterward, she asked for feedback from trusted colleagues, and that buoyed her confidence.

When it was time for the next board meeting, she prepared two versions of her content: a detailed version PowerPoint deck that she turned in ahead of time, and another shortened, high-level printout as a handout. This made her feel safe that if board members dove into the details, she could point them to the read-ahead version. Forgoing the memorization, she allowed herself to speak more naturally and extemporaneously. Freed of the need to make every sentence perfect, she used her energy to show what she really cared about and felt more agile on her feet. Again, she asked a trusted colleague for feedback and modified her approach from there.

This iterative process went through a few rounds: try new actions, get feedback, adjust assumptions, make modifications, adopt new behaviors, and repeat. Eventually, Rebecca changed her assumption permanently, recognizing that she brought tremendous value to the board based on her wealth of experience, not on her efforts to deliver with perfection. This shift allowed her to see and minimize the nervousness and stress that was undermining her effectiveness. Consequently, the CEO and board members also shifted their assumptions about Rebecca.

Rebecca's example shows how we can grow if we are willing to pause and explore our underlying thinking. You can do the same. First, remember that you have a choice in your reaction. Nothing is automatic except your thinking, and that's yours to change. When you feel stress coming on, question your assumptions:

- What's an alternative way to describe this same situation?
- What would feeling confidence do for your response?
- How would [insert colleague's name whom you admire] handle this?

PAUSE AND HIT RESET

More and more, I'm seeing mindfulness included among the offerings in leadership programs around the world. Companies such as Google, Intel, IBM, and SAP have incorporated leadership trainings on how to be more mindful, present, productive, relaxed, and happy.[8] Google has had such positive results with their mindfulness trainings that they've launched the Search Inside Yourself Institute to spread it to other organizations.

Now, not every company is ready to embrace the word "mindfulness." Some use terms like "focused attention," "stress management," or "sustainability." But increasingly, the concept is being offered and readily accepted by leaders.

Scott Eblin calls mindfulness "awareness plus intention." When we're trying to get out of a stress event or a chronic state of overwhelm, it can have a major impact in a short amount of time. Mindfulness practice doesn't require a deep dive into a new age lifestyle. Just selecting a few activities can take us far on our goal to reduce overwhelm.

We can use mindfulness either preventatively on a regular basis or to catch ourselves in the moment. Especially before trying to connect with others in a meaningful way, and certainly before every Inspire Path conversation, it's to your advantage to clear out the stressful energy and to refocus yourself. This stimulates our parasympathetic nervous system—as Eblin puts it, "rest and digest"—and turns off our sympathetic nervous system of "fight or flight." Here are some ways to get into a calmer mindset in as little as a few minutes:

Center and breathe

When stressed, the body assumes a tense posture from our faces to our legs. By centering we are literally bringing our body back to a centered, more neutral state. Try sitting in your chair with feet flat on the ground, back straight, and arms open to your sides. Breathe in four counts and out four counts several times. You're not only relaxing your body, you are oxygenating your brain and lowering your blood pressure. The sage advice to take deep breaths is scientifically proven to stimulate your parasympathetic nervous system.[9]

Take short breaks

Business book author, lecturer, and CEO of The Energy Project Tony Schwartz posits that all too often we ignore the rhythm to our days. Citing sleep researchers, he states that our bodies are designed to work in ninety-minute increments before needing a mental or physical break. Our bodies give us signals—such as hunger, fatigue, or loss of focus—that we need to refresh ourselves. Many of us override these signals through caffeine or sugary foods, and lock our brains into a stress-producing fight or flight zone to get our work done.[10] Conversely, if we want to be more productive, we actually need to cease work at regular intervals.

Change your location

Many people do this absentmindedly when they need a break—they go to get a drink or to the bathroom or for a walk down the hall. Try moving your location mindfully. Make yourself get up from your desk and sit in another chair in your office, or walk to a different room. A simple change of surroundings can reignite your energy and creativity.

Engage your body

Our body holds our stress. By using it in a different way, we can release some of it. Stand up and take a stretch, go for a walk, or even hit the gym if you can. If you can't get up, close your eyes and focus on relaxing your muscles, from your head to your feet.

Focus on gratitude

There's an entire body of research around how gratitude affects our well-being and health. When we contemplate what we're grateful for, we get a hit of dopamine, the brain's pleasure chemical. This feels good, and it creates a virtuous cycle. Because we only have so much mental energy and focus available to us, when we're focused on the good stuff, there's less room for the bad. To put this into practice, when you feel overwhelmed or stressed, stop and consider what you're grateful for. Take a couple of minutes, practice deep breathing, and put the object of your gratitude in your mind's eye.

USE SITUATIONAL INTENTIONS

If you've read anything I've written or seen me speak in the past ten years, there's a good chance you have heard me discuss intention. In my work helping leaders to have a more compelling, clear, and authentic presence, I have found using intention to be the linchpin. When we pause—even for as little as a few moments—and truly focus on what we're trying to impart then we open up a range of opportunities for ourselves that were lying dormant.

In *The Power of Presence* I spend the first third of the book on crafting and using intentions. There are different ways to use intention, both long-term in determining what we want to stand for, and short-term in figuring out our intention for a particular situation. For our purposes in this book on inspirational communications, and this chapter on overwhelm, I'm going to focus on the fastest shortcut with a big payback: situational intentions.

Situational intentions are in-the-moment calibrations to get your head around your real purpose in communicating. They are a simple yet powerful timeout. Even in a few moments, they can transform a conversation. For Inspire Path conversations, situational intentions change the entire dynamic. They use the space that Frankl mentions, or the pause we discussed in Chapter 1. Situational intentions are a stop to reset the direction.

Situational intentions are in-the-moment pauses to consider the emotion we are trying to impart.

Here's how to use them. Before any important interpersonal exchange, first pause and consider:

How do I want my audience to feel?
How do I need to show up to put that feeling in the room?

The operative word is "feel." We process people emotionally first, then fill in the blanks with logic. When you leave a meeting after hearing a leader speak, you describe your reaction based on how you felt about it: "I was excited/concerned/skeptical/unsure about that." This emotion is conveyed by you and retrieved by another. We can't make someone else feel something that we're not showing. I can't make you excited if I approach you looking distracted and tired. I can't get you to take a change initiative seriously if I look like I have not bought in.

When I introduce this concept to my clients, what I hear most often is that they never really thought about it that way. They are running full-tilt from meeting to meeting without pausing to take a breath let alone reflecting on an emotional intention. That's exactly why this concept is so critical, especially in a chapter about overwhelm. When we take this moment to reorient our thinking, center our energy, and focus on an intention, we make ourselves far more present to the person in front of us.

Many clients find that they are best able to get themselves out of overwhelm, connect, and be present when they combine a few of these ideas. The next time you have an important conversation and want to connect, give yourself ten minutes to get your head in the game. Shut your door, move away from your desk, take a few deep breaths, and consider your intention for the upcoming interaction. Hold it in your mind's eye for a few minutes. You will show up differently and have a more connected conversation as a result. It's a perfect way to start an Inspire Path conversation.

CHALLENGE YOUR HAIR-ON-FIRE STORIES

The pace of our lives and our work can feel manic. Some of us are in a constant state of overwhelm and ready to snap. Others succumb to those days or periods where we can't get out from underneath the expectations so we try to hunker down and push through it. If you're a leader, no matter how busy you feel, you still need to be a connected and inspiring presence for others. That's something that can never be delegated or postponed. Being able to get yourself present quickly, strategically, and methodically will serve you, and those around you, in a multitude of ways.

A friend once told me, "The work is infinite but your time is finite." This is exquisitely true in our times. You could work 24/7 and still have plenty to do. So then it becomes about choices: how you work, what you prioritize, who you want to be. When we're on chronic overload, we easily buy into our own stories. We seek to reinforce what we've already told ourselves, even when it hurts us. So, challenge your own stories about what "has to be" or what you "need to do." All the leaders I've worked with who have changed their presence have first changed their perspective. And as my personal story of overwhelm in the beginning shows, we need rewrites along the way.

TAKEAWAYS

FROM CHAPTER 2

⊙ With the pace of today's work, it's common for people to be in near-constant overwhelm, which forces our bodies into a fight-or-flight response.

⊙ When we're in overwhelm, we're not inspiring anyone. In fact, people's natural instinct is to distance themselves from someone who seems frenetic.

⊙ Stress can cause us to devolve into fear-based behavior. We're inspiring to others when we come from a place of positivity and abundance.

⊙ If we want to get out of overwhelm, we first need to challenge our assumptions rather than jumping to try new strategies. When we engage in this "double loop learning" then more possibilities open to us.

⊙ It doesn't take a lot of time to get to a place of being centered and connected before a conversation. Try deep breathing, instituting short breaks, changing your location, engaging your body, focusing on gratitude, and using situational intentions.

CHAPTER 3

TRICKING YOUR BRAIN
TO OPEN YOUR MIND

When I was twenty-eight, I quit my job and started my first business. I began on my own, offering marketing and communications consulting services to the D.C. area's then-burgeoning technology market. Within a year I had a partner, several employees, a solid client base, and a real office. I was young, ambitious, naïve, and hardworking, with the benefit of great timing as the market grew. I also had one more quality that I felt contributed to my success: I loved to solve problems.

As an entrepreneur—and especially an inexperienced one—the world is one problem after another. You have to find clients, keep clients, and get employees on board when you have little to offer. You have to set up an organizational structure, manage cash flow, and figure out how to limit your risk. Regularly, a client asks for something you've never done before—something you may never have even heard of. In a client service business, and especially a high-visibility one like public relations and marketing, you have to manage a host of political and ego-driven client issues.

Actually liking to solve problems helped me feel excitement and accomplishment in an otherwise stressful environment of unknowns. As

I solved more problems and they began to repeat, I got better at it. I could solve problems faster, and attack larger ones. My team members brought me more of them—even ones they could be solving on their own. We established ways to handle common problems, and rather than recreating the wheel we tried to institutionalize solutions.

Everything seemed great; we were cooking. Then about two years in, cracks began to appear. We hit a wall around innovation. We weren't providing fresh ideas, and clients began to complain about it. Thinking that new people equal new ideas, we hired new people. But those new hires quickly learned to fit into our model by following our set processes and kicking the problems up to the partners to solve.

You can probably guess the culprit—me. My love of problem-solving was limiting the company. It wasn't that we lacked new ideas. We had plenty of talented people, but there was no way for innovation to take hold. The more problems I experienced, and the more repetitive they became, the fewer new ideas were getting into the system. Sure, I got faster, but the range of possibilities shrunk—exactly the opposite of what a company that's trying to grow and innovate wants. My mind was narrowing, and because there was no incentive for other people to bring fresh ideas, we were stagnating. (We eventually fixed this, but it took a major overhaul of our roles.)

I've seen this dynamic play out repeatedly with other entrepreneurs and corporate leaders. Perhaps people self-select into these leadership roles because they do love the challenge of solving problems. At first, they bring a trove of new ideas and solutions. Once they get to a place of competency though, without an intentional effort to continually expand their range of thinking, their own success ends up limiting them.

Or as the playwright George Bernard Shaw put it: "Those who cannot change their minds cannot change anything."

We'd like to believe that our thinking expands with experience and age. Isn't that what the elusive wisdom is all about? In fact, opening our minds gets harder as we get better at things. Our thinking calcifies with success and experience.[1]

Opening our minds gets harder as we get better at things. Our thinking calcifies with success and experience.

Researchers at Loyola University in Chicago tested a phenomenon that they called "earned dogmatism." According to the earned dogmatism hypothesis, people who believe they are experts become less open-minded and more dogmatic in their thinking. In one experiment, the researchers had study participants answer political questions. One group got the easy questions like "Who is the current president?" and one group got the harder ones, such as "Who was Nixon's original vice president?" Those who had the easy test were told they aced it, while those with the difficult test were told they performed poorly.

Then all participants were asked to rate themselves on a series of statements to measure open-mindedness such as, "I am open to considering other political viewpoints." The participants who had the easy questions were *more* close-minded and certain when asked about their political beliefs.

The findings were replicated across six studies, of varying topics. When participants were made to feel they were experts, they overly invested in their own opinions. They were more likely to believe they were right and less likely to admit they didn't know an answer.

This fascinating study shows that not only do true experts narrow their thinking, but so do those whom researchers just made to *feel* were experts. When people believe they have the right answer, they stop considering any other alternatives.

Think about how this plays out at work. Many leaders have risen to a position of success, then are surrounded by people who praise them for their judgment and results. Just like in my own example, the more we think we know, the less we listen and consider alternative viewpoints. We close our minds, and the dynamic becomes a trap.

OPEN-MINDEDNESS AND BEING PRESENT

As the name implies, our open-mindedness shows how open we are to the thoughts and presence of others. We're more present if we're more open-minded. And if we're more present, we're more inspiring. In my research on inspiring leaders, I heard repeatedly that those who inspire us are right there with us, not judging, not pushing, but trying to understand where we're coming from. Even if they are experts, they don't force their advice on us, but help us to make our own decisions. They guide, but they don't dictate.

Those who inspire us are right there with us, not judging, not pushing, but trying to understand where we're coming from.

Sounds like a great person to know or be, right?

Open-mindedness is seen as a universal virtue. No one sets a New Year's resolution to become more close-minded (unless they want fewer friends to celebrate with next year). Having an open mind is equated with approachability, friendliness, and being nonjudgmental. Most of us would say we are open-minded—and we're quick to point out when we think others aren't.

If only open-mindedness were that easy. Unfortunately, our brains are rigged against us. It's not just success that gets in the way of an open mind, but our basic brain functioning.

WHY YOU NEED A CROWBAR
TO OPEN YOUR MIND

We have heard lovely stories about how much horsepower we have sitting on top of our necks, if only we could use it fully. Our brains are described as powerhouses and supercomputers, with an amazing capacity to take in data, retain it, and find connections between disparate concepts.

While it may be true that our brains are highly capable, neuroscientists and behavioral economists have spent the past decade also proving that we are "cognitive misers." Because the brain's primary goal is efficiency, it creates a myriad of shortcuts for us to simplify our thinking so we can reduce our energy burn. This is terrific news when we're driving to work, as we barely have to think about how to get there. But it's not so good when we make knee-jerk assumptions about Bob in accounting without even knowing that we're doing it.

Because the brain's primary goal is efficiency, it creates a myriad of shortcuts for us to simplify our thinking.

One of my favorite thought leaders on this topic is Daniel Kahneman, Princeton University professor, renowned researcher, winner of the Nobel Prize in Economic Sciences, and author of several books including, *Thinking, Fast and Slow*. Kahneman brilliantly condenses and simplifies what is happening to us when we attempt to understand and make decisions (thus making his readers' brains happy). It says a lot that *Thinking, Fast and Slow*, clocking in at nearly 500 dense pages, was a *New York Times* bestseller. The book describes our complicated brain functioning in a way that's incredibly accessible and useful for anyone.[2]

Kahneman breaks down our thinking into two functions: System 1 and System 2:

- **System 1** thinking is automatic and quick, requiring little to no effort. It happens without our even realizing we're thinking. This is how you know how to read, or to jump out of the way of an oncoming car. System 1 adapts from experience. Once you know how to count, you can't unlearn it.

- **System 2** thinking takes effort. It's associated with concentration, decisionmaking, and analysis. It requires attention, and when that's taken away, System 2 is disrupted. If you were studying for a test or writing a speech, you'd be using System 2 thinking. Though both systems are always at work, in general, System 2 takes the suggestions of System 1 without challenge. It's only when System 1 has a problem that System 2 jumps in.

This interplay allows us to function in a way that's not overly taxing. System 2 takes energy, and even makes us blind to other factors. When all of our attention is on one thing, then we miss everything else happening around us. An episode of the Nat Geo show *Brain Games* demonstrates this perfectly, by asking viewers to focus on counting the intricate movements of dancers. All the while people in outlandish animal costumes are walking back and forth on the stage. Viewers are so focused on the dance steps that they don't even see the costumed people until the slow-motion recap. (This is similar to the 1999 study many have seen on *inattentional blindness*, where viewers focus on basketballs being passed and miss a large gorilla. The research led to a book by Christopher Chabris and Daniel Simons called, aptly, *The Invisible Gorilla*.)

System 1 is fast, but it's far from accurate. It's filled with biases: cultural, personal, and learned. It also can't be turned off. The only thing we can do is understand what's happening in our thinking, and prompt System 2 to boot up when we need it. This is essentially why Kahneman wrote the book—to take our unconscious conditioning and teach us how to make conscious choices.

We have a host of unconscious biases that gum up our thinking and cause us to react in often close-minded ways. Here are a few that occur frequently in typical business settings:

- **Anchoring:** We rely too much on the first piece of information we receive about a person, a product, a number, or just about anything—and then judge subsequent interactions in relation to that first judgment. This is why those who throw out the first number in a negotiation are more likely to get closer to what they want, and why first impressions are hard to overcome.[3]

- **Confirmation Bias:** We seek out information that confirms what we're already thinking. In essence, we are using System 2 to bolster System 1's first impression. This plays out in hiring, when we inflate the qualifications of someone who seems most like us, or has come recommended from a friend.

- **Arbitrary Coherence:** Related to anchoring, but perhaps even more troubling, even data that's entirely irrelevant to what we're determining can influence our decision. Duke University professor Dan Ariely performed a study where he asked people to write down the last two digits of their social security numbers, then write down what they'd be willing to pay for a number of consumer items. Participants with higher two-digit numbers submitted bids that were 60 to 120 percent higher.[4]

- **Recency Bias:** We overvalue information from the recent past, and assume that it will continue in the future. This is a common complaint about performance reviews, where evaluators rely on the near past to explain an employee's performance over the course of an entire year. Overcoming this is of particular importance in financial markets, where traders can rely on a stock's last move, and overlook larger trends.

- **Correspondence Bias:** We assign meaning to people's behavior in an automatic way, and assume that the behavior can be explained by someone's personality or character. If a colleague turns in work late, then he's lazy. If your student fails a test, then she isn't smart enough. If your date doesn't call you again, then he's a player. Now here's where it gets interesting. When we look at our own behavior, we attribute it not to character, but to the situation. Our work is late because we were overloaded. If we fail a test, then the questions were unfair. If we don't call a date again, it must have slipped our mind. In reality, research psychologists tell us emphatically that people's behavior is a poor predictor of their intent, so we're jumping to a lot of erroneous conclusions.[5]

We have a host of biases that gum up our thinking, all below our consciousness.

Psychologists have identified many more such biases. All this is to say, that System 1 has some serious bugs. In fact, none of us are open-minded. If we want to grow in this area, we have to make an effort to understand our thinking, and then to challenge it. We're better off going into a situation *knowing* that we're prone to knee-jerk, unconscious reactions. Then we can begin to institute some new approaches, and train our brains to think differently.

LET'S NOT FORGET ABOUT INFLUENCE

Now that we've tapped into the forces inside of us that limit our ability to think expansively, it's worth spending a few paragraphs discussing the external or social factors that also influence us. Just like System 1, these factors prey on our unconscious, and gently sway our behavior without conscious control. Perhaps the most well-known source on influence is Robert Cialdini, psychology professor, researcher, and author of *Influence: Science and Practice.*[6] In *Influence,* Cialdini breaks down the six elements of influence that drive our behavior:

- **Reciprocation:** We feel compelled to respond if someone has done a favor, whether real or perceived. If your colleague sticks her neck out for you, you're more likely to be influenced by her in the future.

- **Commitment and consistency:** If we commit to an idea, especially in public, we're more likely to act in alignment with that commitment. This is why stating goals out loud to others, like a plan to lose weight, influences our behavior to stick with it.
- **Social proof:** We conform to the behavior of those around us. If your colleagues don't seem to care about getting expense reports in on time, you won't either. This is also why peer pressure gets people in trouble.
- **Authority:** We act in accordance with those we deem to be in positions of authority, such as our bosses. You can see this in the effectiveness of advertising featuring fake doctors wearing lab coats.
- **Liking:** We're more persuaded by people we like, and who seem similar to us. This explains all of the bias research around hiring people who look like us and come from similar backgrounds.
- **Scarcity:** If we believe something is running out or may go away, we're more likely to act. This explains one-day-only sales and why there's never any bread left in supermarkets just before a snowstorm.

It doesn't take much to recognize these forces at work in us. We fall into these logic traps repeatedly and unconsciously. Sometimes they serve us, but often they work against us. Certainly no one sets out to be a close-minded automaton guided by cognitive biases and social influences. Yet, we often are that bound by automaticity.

Luckily, we can kick in our trusty System 2 at any time and start questioning our thinking. Being able to understand, examine, and even counter the influences on our thoughts and behavior enables us to expand our thinking and our range of motion. We can't do what we can't see. Being open-minded means being able to broaden our lens, so we can see a fuller picture of others and ourselves.

CONCEPT IN ACTION

INSPIRING WITH
OPEN-MINDEDNESS

Inspire Path conversations require us to engage consciously at a deeper level, with presence and open-mindedness. We all know how to do it. We simply need to choose to show up in a different way.

Many leaders feel that people come to them every day, all day, looking for clear, direct answers. There are times when this is the right approach. Make a decision and move on. But more often, leaders need to inspire action in others, and help influence another's thinking. Just as in the story about starting my own business that opened this chapter, if we do all the thinking, then we're not creating a space for others to add their own marks. And we certainly don't want to reinforce a dynamic that narrows an organization's thinking by an overreliance on a few key people.

If we do the thinking, then we're not creating a space for others to make their mark.

Therefore, as you read these next suggestions for how to be more open-minded, be sure to keep your own mind open! Think about all the conversations you have where you want to motivate, inspire, connect, and encourage. Those are exactly the times to consider how you might incorporate some of these approaches.

USE A "PRE-MORTEM"

Often, conversations in which we need to inspire come with high stakes. We hope to sell our vision to a room of investors, or convince a customer to buy our product. We want to turn around a challenging employee, or get a team to work harder. These interactions can trigger stress and make us lose our composure. One of the ways we can keep ourselves in a calm, open-minded stance is to assume ahead of time that we're going to be triggered and our thinking will get cloudy—and prepare with what neuroscientist Daniel Levitin calls a "pre-mortem."[7]

We're already good at doing postmortems. Who hasn't bungled an important conversation and then afterward ruminated on what went wrong? The pre-mortem idea is to know yourself well enough to understand what biases will kick in, what triggers could flare, what influences you're susceptible to, and what you'll do ahead of time to remain present, focused, and open-minded.

For example, a client of mine knew that whenever he spoke to the board he would get overly nervous and deferential to authority, which would get in the way of being able to deliver tough information confidently. By knowing this ahead of time, he was prepared with a plan *while his thinking was still clear.* In the meeting, when he could feel himself starting to go down that hole, he knew to take a deep breath and focus on providing short, direct answers rather than rambling in an effort to curry favor.

ASK OPEN QUESTIONS

If you want to have an open mind, and open the minds of others, learn how to ask open questions. Most questions that we ask are close-ended fact-finders starting with "Why . . ." or "Did . . ." Primarily, they elicit right-or-wrong answers, and they come across as judgmental. When someone asks us why we did what we did, we go into defensive mode.

If I were to ask you, "Why did you buy this book?" you'd probably feel like you have to explain yourself. (Thanks for buying it, by the way.)

On the other hand, open-ended questions encourage minds to wander. Coming from a place of curiosity about the other person, they can be illuminating for both sides of the conversation.

When we feel judged we shut down. When we feel someone is genuinely interested in our thinking, then we open up. As a plus, when we ask open questions, and listen closely for other people's thought processes, we learn a great deal about them and the situation. See the examples below of typical closed versus open questions:

CLOSED QUESTIONS	OPEN QUESTIONS
Why are you here?	What brings you here?
Why did this happen?	What factors led to this place?
Who was responsible?	How did this come about?
Did you consider trying it this way?	What would you do, if you could do anything?
Do you see the problem?	How is the view from your vantage point?
Do you know what you're going to do?	What's possible?

When you're in Inspire Path conversations, your job is to open your own mind, and to help the other person expand his as well. Even if you have an opinion of what you want him to do, you're more likely to get a commitment if he feels ownership of the idea. We're most influential when we're creating the space for others to create their own insights.

USE THE NATO APPROACH:
NOT ATTACHED TO OUTCOME

In our culture, we try to control just about anything we can. We equate control, stress, and effort with desire. If we want something badly enough, then we'll work hard to make it turn out the way we want. On the flip side, we hate being controlled by someone else. If we're in a conversation where we feel manipulated, we lose trust and get protective fast.

When someone listens to us without trying to game the outcome, it feels like a gift. This is why executives hire coaches—we're often the only people in their lives who don't have a stake in their decisions.

When someone listens to us without trying to game the outcome, it feels like a gift.

In conversations that matter to us then, our first impulse can be to control them in order to achieve our desired outcome. The larger the audience, the more effort people usually put into preparing—whether or not the communication event is actually more important. Certainly for any Inspire Path conversation, we care about what happens! However, we can achieve more if we loosen our grip on the outcome, and give the conversation space to play out in its own way.

I love the acronym NATO, for *not attached to outcome*, which is loosely based on a Buddhist concept that the origin of suffering is attachment to our desires. NATO is a little playful and memorable, and gaining some renown, even finding a spot in the Urban Dictionary. But there's great power behind it. When we want something badly enough, we hold onto it tightly. And that limits our range of motion. When we can let go of a particular outcome or expectation, it can free us up to be open and to create more opportunity.

We usually can't control the entire outcome anyway: That's an illusion. When human beings interact, anything can happen. All we can control is our reaction to the outcome. That doesn't mean that we don't care, shouldn't try our best, or shouldn't prepare. It means that we do all that we can, leave room for possibilities, and accept that the cards will play out as they will.

There's an ancient Chinese saying: "Come with an empty cup." In other words, we can't learn if our cup is already full with our own answers. If we come with an empty cup, we empty our minds of what *should* happen, and provide room for what *can* happen.

EMBRACE "I DON'T KNOW"

From our youngest days, we are rewarded for having the right answers. We raise our hand first in school, and the teacher praises us. Then we go to work where we get recognized for our fast responses and quick thinking. If we continue to rise, sooner or later we get into a position where we're asked something that we don't know. This is inevitable, as we're responsible for a wider span of activities, with more complexity, and we can't possibly know everything.

In some organizations where I've worked, people live in abject fear that someone senior to them will ask a question that they can't answer. You can guess that these are also environments where innovation is an issue—where people are so worried about knowing everything that they can't take risks or delegate properly. These are not fun places to work.

To be open-minded, we have to admit that there are things we don't know. Now yes, I'm sure we all agree that's true. But we also have to *act* as if it's true. Embracing uncertainty allows us to be that empty cup that creates room for someone else's ideas.

Embracing uncertainty and saying "I don't know" invites outside thinking. It also shows courage.

Leaders who are unafraid of saying, "I don't know" invite outside thinking. It shows courage, not weakness. Not having all the answers creates an invitation to others. And it can even start a revolution of innovation.

In her groundbreaking book, *MindSet*, Stanford University psychologist Carol Dweck has created an entire movement that's shaping institutions from Fortune 50 corporations to preschools.[8] Her work is based on decades of research into achievement and success. She found that people are most resilient and successful when they develop a *growth mindset*—the belief that basic abilities can be developed through effort and hard work. Those with a growth mindset expect to work hard for mastery, and don't take it personally when challenges arise. The opposite approach, a *fixed mindset*, is the belief that abilities are based on intelligence or talents. Instead of stretching to grow, those with a fixed mindset play it safe to ensure their intelligence is never challenged—and they wilt in the face of difficulties.

Embracing "I don't know" encourages a growth mindset. The follow up to it is, "let's find out." When leaders are also learners, their teams and organizations benefit because the behavior models a collective growth mindset that says, "Never stop improving."

IF YOU CAN'T AGREE, ACKNOWLEDGE

It's easy to forget how the concept of validation is a game-changer in interpersonal relationships. The simple act of saying "I get you" or "I see where you're coming from" can literally shift the conversation in an instant.

Acknowledgment, however, can be a challenge when we don't actually agree with what the other person is saying. If we're trying to inspire a new customer to buy our software product, and the customer feels that the product isn't as good as the competition, our first instinct is to push back about the reasons that they're wrong. But in this instance, when we push, they retreat, because we have invalidated their concerns. Another approach is to acknowledge what the customer has said—even if it's flat out wrong. *I understand that, from where you sit, it seems that our product lags behind. I respect your opinion.* Or: *Many people share your initial impression of our product, as we've not gotten our message out there. I hope to gradually change that.* When we acknowledge, we create a space to have a different conversation with an open mind, one that feels more on equal terms.

I've worked with many clients around this issue of acknowledgment. A few years ago, one client (let's call him Dave) was about to lose his top employee to a competitor. The employee felt that he didn't have growth potential at the company. Dave strongly disagreed and wanted the employee to feel that was not the case. They had a few conversations; Dave sold hard, but wasn't able to get the employee to agree to stay. Finally, Dave approached the employee with an open mind, acknowledging why he might feel that way based on past experience. Rather than a competition of perspectives, they agreed to approach the situation together. With Dave seeking to understand, the employee felt freer to think more broadly. Only then could Dave turn the conversation around. In the end, the employee stayed with Dave's full support to ensure his future success.

Acknowledging what's true for someone else—even if it's not true for you—is a good leadership skill to hone. It makes conversations less confrontational, and gets both parties to the same side of the table.

CREATE SPACE
TO LET YOUR MIND WANDER

To end this chapter I'll go back to the beginning of this section on being present. In our frenetic, connected world we have scant time to be with our thoughts. We have access to more information than we could have dreamed of a few decades ago, yet less time to fully absorb it. Having an open mind requires time to process our thoughts. If we don't make time for it, no one else is going to do it for us.

If you want to be present in important conversations, you may want to start by being present in conversations with yourself. It's exceedingly important for leaders—and really for anyone—to have time to let our minds go.

To be present to conversations with others, we first have to be present to conversations with ourselves.

When is your true quiet time to think? How do you contemplate and integrate new information that you've learned? Where is your designated space to reflect?

Incorporating even small amounts of reflection time changes my clients' lives dramatically. The time commitment doesn't have to be long. Several years ago, I began consciously using drive time to think. I stopped making phone calls or turning on music. I use the time to be in quiet. Now, instead of hating to drive I've come to enjoy it as important time. This works for me. Figure out what works for you. Schedule bi-monthly strategy sessions with yourself, get up a half-hour earlier to think through your day, or do a full-week retreat. See what opens up for you when you create the space and allow yourself to step into it. And be NATO about it.

TAKEAWAYS

FROM CHAPTER 3

- ◉ We can't open someone else's mind if ours is closed. When we cultivate an open mind, we create a learning space that allows others to expand their own thinking.

- ◉ Our thinking calcifies with success and experience. We develop "earned dogmatism" in which people who believe they are experts become less open-minded and more dogmatic in their thinking.

- ◉ Our brains are cognitive misers, and have developed a series of shortcuts to limit our deep thinking in order to save energy. Consider our cognitive functions as Kahneman's System 1 and System 2. System 1 is automatic and can't be turned off. System 1 has numerous cognitive biases that limit our thinking and judgment, and operate underneath our consciousness. System 2 is our more deliberate, logical, focused attention, and it kicks in only when System 1 can't handle it alone.

- ◉ In addition to cognitive limitations, we are also influenced by social factors such as reciprocity, commitment and consistency, social proof, authority, liking, and scarcity.

- ◉ In order to cultivate an open mind and encourage expansive thinking in others, we need to have a plan. Using a "pre-mortem," asking curious questions, detaching from the outcome, being able to say "I don't know," and setting time for spacious thinking can help us show and nurture an open-minded approach.

PERSONAL

PUTTING
YOURSELF
INTO IT

CHAPTER 4

FIRST, KEEP IT REAL

One of the most common pieces of early career advice most people receive is to not take work personally. It's as if we're all supposed to strap on bulletproof vests, so that when we have setbacks, when we mess up or get negative feedback, we can feel the impact but not be affected. We're to adopt a posture somewhere between battle-tested stoicism and generalized detachment.

As nearly all of us are indoctrinated into the working world this way, it causes a struggle when we meet with a popular imperative for leadership: to be authentic. Um, aren't these ideas in conflict? How can I be fully myself when I'm not supposed to let them see me sweat? How do I balance the messages I'm tasked to deliver with what I actually feel about them? Is it possible to be too authentic at work?

The irony is that work is extremely personal, no matter how we try to manage it. Lots of us spend more time working than just about anything else. We put our heart into our jobs, take personal risks to advance, and put our skills and personalities on the line every day. Work is intensely personal. That's an important element that shouldn't get lost—and I would argue, should even be amplified. We can't inspire without it.

We're moving into the next section of the book, which covers how to be more personal in our communications. In this chapter, we're diving into authenticity, a concept we hear about in leadership circles but aren't always sure what to do about. Authenticity is the epitome of being personal because we're being our true selves. When we're having Inspire Path conversations, authenticity plays a critical role in connection. Your listener looks to you first to see how much you care, and this is what shapes how much he will care. He wants to see that you've bought in before he considers the idea. Your listener might not match your level of commitment, but he won't have any if you don't appear to have it. We all have our BS detectors tuned up, especially when the stakes are high. If you want to move behavior or shape thinking, you need to get personal and stay personal. We're not inspired by fakes, frauds, blowhards, blusterers, or even by those who play it too close to the vest. We need to see the real deal.

Authenticity seems to fly in the face of the impassiveness we've been trained to adopt at work. But people look to you to see how much you care, and this shapes how much they will care.

THE AGE OF AUTHENTICITY

In 2003, former CEO of Medtronic and Harvard management professor Bill George published *Authentic Leadership*, which popularized the theory that the best leaders bring their full selves to the task. George explains authentic leadership this way:

Authentic leaders use their natural abilities, but they also recognize their shortcomings, and work hard to overcome them. They lead with purpose, meaning, and values. They build enduring relationships with people. Others follow them because they know where they stand. They are consistent and self-disciplined. When their principles are tested, they refuse to compromise. Authentic leaders are dedicated to developing themselves because they know that becoming a leader takes a lifetime of work.[1]

Throughout the 2000s, there's been a steady drumbeat of research and literature about how authentic leadership produces better outcomes for teams and companies, and how to define and explain what authentic leaders actually do.[2] There's a sincere desire to prove that being an engaged and inspirational leader actually does lead to good results, and to help leaders learn what they can do differently.

While researchers research, popular culture has wholeheartedly embraced the idea of authentic leadership. People who are real, speak the truth, and talk from the heart are admired. They may display a variety of personality styles, but they come from a place that's real and unique to them. Consider the popularity of figures like Oprah, Pope Francis, Malala Yousafzai, Warren Buffett, or Zappos CEO Tony Hsieh. In fact, people who are seen as authentic leaders dominate Gallup's annual poll of the most admired men and women.[3] Another example of this is the global phenomenon of TED Talks, where experts combine their research with very personal stories. Truth and sincerity are on full display.

We admire those who are real, speak the truth, and talk from the heart.

It's also worth noting that, more than any other demographic, millennials are even more bought into the model of authentic leadership. This age group, who comprise the majority of the workforce and are now rising to management positions, grew up with a different relationship to authority than their Baby Boomer parents, and expect flatter, less directive relationships between leaders and teams.[4]

The expectations for being authentic appear to be going up, not down. Throw in the variety of ways that leaders are seen through their online presence and through social media, and you have intimate touchpoints that just didn't even exist twenty years ago when Gen Xers were entering the workforce. But let's go back to where we started: Even though we buy into the promise of authenticity in the workforce, how to put more of it out there for ourselves is not so cut and dried.

THE MAGIC BALANCING ACT

Authenticity is hard because no one is either always authentic or always inauthentic. Our behavior exists on a continuum; we decide from moment to moment what to share and what to show. We also can and do learn how to adjust our authenticity to find the style that works for us at particular points in time. We grow and we change. Herminia Ibarra, professor of organizational behavior at INSEAD business school and author of *Act Like a Leader, Think Like a Leader* explains that there can be a tension between the comfort in our total authenticity and the bravery to try new behaviors on for size. "That takes courage," she writes, "because learning, by definition, starts with unnatural and often superficial behaviors that can make us feel calculating instead of genuine and spontaneous. But the only way to avoid being pigeonholed and ultimately become better leaders is to do the things that a rigidly authentic sense of self would keep us from doing."[5]

She goes on to explain that as we build confidence in new behaviors, it becomes easier to incorporate them as our own, and therefore, part of our authentic selves. She calls it being "adaptively authentic."[6] I believe wholeheartedly in this idea, which plays out in coaching all the time. We adapt to new learning and decide what behaviors to begin and which to shed. We absorb new behaviors into our own repertoire.

Authenticity truly is a balancing act. I spent the earliest part of my career working as a political consultant getting federal candidates elected to office. It was many years ago, but the experience of trying to figure out how to get voters to connect to a candidate was invaluable. It's a tough environment where skepticism and mistrust are high, and time is of the essence. If you can master communications strategy in political campaigns, anything else seems easy by comparison.

In the role of helping candidates communicate, I learned a pivotal lesson that has influenced my work since: People are drawn to those who blend *competency* with *vulnerability*. We knew, and had poll numbers to prove it, that when we could show voters that a candidate had both ability and authenticity then voters would respond positively. We spent countless hours scouring candidate backgrounds for stories that showed their relatability and humanity. All campaigns do this, which is why you know the candidates' back-stories.

People are drawn to those who blend competency with vulnerability.

This lesson is as true in the corporate and public relations spheres as it is in politics. The most compelling leaders blend strength with struggle, power with vulnerability, and steely resolve with a learning approach.

Even though I learned this lesson through experience, there's solid research to back it up. We've known about the *pratfall effect* since the 1960s. According to this concept, people who are seen as competent become more likeable if they show a personal weakness.[7] The pratfall effect has been repeatedly studied through the lens of communications, negotiations, body language, and interpersonal relationships.[8]

So there's a balancing act to have the right amount of authenticity—which can seem like the opposite of being authentic. It's a push and pull. People want to be authentic, but they also need to be strong. It's a tension that's in the background, and can cause us to feel that we'll never get it right.

DOES AUTHENTICITY SCALE?

One of the larger challenges of authentic leadership is how to scale it. You can be an empathetic, funny, kind, inspiring person with your close friends, but that may not translate when you're running a team of a hundred or a company of ten thousand. How do you communicate your authentic self to people who don't even know you? It's a common issue that people face as their audience gets larger and less familiar.

Authenticity may also have to scale, as your audience gets larger and less familiar.

This was the case for one of my clients, whom I'll call Gabe. Gabe had been with his company for decades, working primarily in a satellite office. Known for accomplishing the impossible, he had a loyal, close-knit following of team members and customers who sang his praises. Gabe had a sharp, sarcastic wit and a quick retort for everything. His mind worked fast, he talked faster, and he approached each day as a new challenge to tackle. His team had grown up with him, and had long ago found the person of integrity and caring that existed underneath his curt and efficient manner.

A few years ago, Gabe's company went through a major reorganization. The new executive team was looking for people who could shake up the status quo, and Gabe fit the bill. He relocated to the headquarters where he was given a significant role with hundreds of direct reports. After accomplishing a lot in a short amount of time, he was given even more responsibility and direct reports. And that's when the problems started.

Gabe's peers began to complain that he was leaving them out of decisions, and not operating as a team player. When he would give a quick email response or delegate a task, he was accused of being dismissive. The new people on Gabe's team began aligning into factions—those who were with him and those who wanted him gone. The more the CEO showered praise on Gabe, the worse the sniping got. He was accused of being out for himself and untrustworthy. Since this had never happened in Gabe's entire career, he was floored. He tried to reach out to people but found every action on his part was interpreted negatively. Why couldn't people see his true intentions? How could the strategy of being himself—which had worked beautifully up until now—backfire? In this new position, he felt that people didn't know him at all.

Gabe had a scaling problem. With his long-term colleagues, his authentic self was appreciated and understood. But when he moved into an unfamiliar environment, people picked up dismissive cues that were in direct conflict with Gabe's intention of inclusion. He was right: People didn't know him. And because they believed they had him figured out, they didn't care to correct the impression.

One famous example of this inability to scale one's personality is Al Gore. When Gore ran for president in 2000, he was routinely mocked for being wooden, boring, and robotic. He was characterized as a humorless talking head. A Pew Research poll found the number one adjective associated with Gore was "boring." In another poll by CNN, 65 percent of respondents said that he was not inspiring.[9] For those in political circles, this was confounding. He had a reputation for being witty, personable, and deeply passionate about causes. People who worked with him talked about his sense of humor. In the Senate, he was seen as a good guy who was well-liked by colleagues. How did all of that get lost?

We all know the story. Gore lost the election, and after much soul searching, set out to advance his cause of fighting climate change, eventually starring in the 2006 documentary *An Inconvenient Truth*. Almost overnight, Gore went from being a stiff policy wonk to one of the most inspiring figures in the sustainability movement. Winner of a Nobel

Peace Prize, a Grammy, and an Oscar, Gore found himself mobbed at film festivals and featured at events with rock stars.[10] All of a sudden, people seemed to "get" Al Gore and see him for who he really was. Love him or hate him, no one was calling him a robot anymore.

There were several reasons for Gore's transformation. Certainly one is that the country became open to the issue of global warming. But beyond that, Gore's approach didn't change all that much. What did change was his ability to project authenticity. We saw him, in talk after talk, put his heart on the line. We could see the person behind the slides and the policy talk—and that's what people gravitated toward. Today, he's still traveling the globe as a transformational leader in the sustainability movement.

So that's Al Gore. But what about my client Gabe? The situation was certainly on a smaller scale, but the core issue was the same. He needed to get clearer around his own values, and then to ensure that they were being translated through his words and his actions. This meant working on his authenticity both *internalized* and *externalized*. It's not enough to have one or the other. We may have the best intentions, but because perception becomes reality we must communicate those intentions. On the other hand, we can also say the right words, but if they don't touch upon our core beliefs, then the dialogue is hollow.

Authenticity can be looked at as both an internal and an external trait.

To bring that kind of authenticity, Gabe incorporated many of the ideas that follow in the upcoming "concept in action" section. Gabe's situation is one example of communicating authentically. Sometimes, like with Gabe, it's about communicating authentically to a team or to corporate leadership. Other times it's about how to convey authenticity and make a personal connection to an audience in a public speaking environment. Or it could be about reaching someone individually.

These are all conversations that count. Authentically connecting matters tremendously.

CONCEPT IN ACTION

AUTHENTICITY FROM THE INSIDE OUT

As we discussed, communicating authentically can be tricky. It's not simply flipping on a switch, but engaging in a continuum of behaviors. It's helpful to approach this as a two-step process: authenticity internalized and authenticity externalized. I suggest that you start with the internal piece and then move into how to translate that to the external. This model offers a way to put the concept of leading with more authenticity into practice.

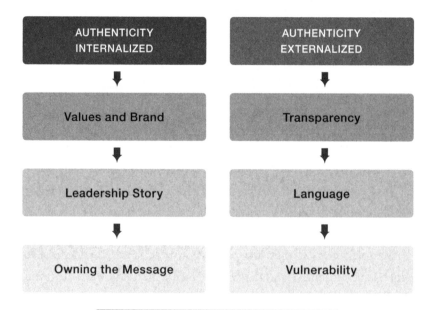

Figure 4.1: Authenticity Infographic

AUTHENTICITY INTERNALIZED

It may sound redundant or even counterproductive to discuss how to be more internally authentic, but stay with me. Typically, we allow the busyness of our days and the urgency of our tasks to obscure our actual, deep-down beliefs and feelings. When we are attempting to make a true connection with someone else, we first should send out a beaming, accurate light that allows another to see our intentions and motivations clearly. When we aren't clear about what we stand for and where we're coming from, then we're opening up the conversation to miscommunication and misinterpretation. By getting our values clear, embracing our story, and owning our message, we can come across with heightened clarity.

To truly connect with someone else, we need to send out a beaming and accurate light that allows them to see our intentions and motivations clearly.

KNOW YOUR VALUES
AND DETERMINE YOUR BRAND

One of the places I start with clients is to provide a simple process for them to understand their personal presence brands. I can't help someone show up with clarity if I don't first understand what he or she is trying to convey. I can't tell people what values to project—only they can do that. Most leaders don't do this at all, and if they do, it's not in actionable form.

The great news is that this process—which is the cornerstone to consistent authenticity and presence—can take less than an hour. Here's all you need to do:

1. List your 10 most cherished values. How do you want others to view you? What do you want your legacy to be? What makes you proud of yourself?

2. Narrow that list down to your top five values that are critical to your self-image. These five are core to who you are, and it would really sting if someone said that you didn't embody these values.

3. Come up with a key phrase or image that evokes that list of five values. This can be a person you admire, a song lyric, a place, a quote, an acronym—anything you want. The most important thing is that it's something that you can remember and keep at the top of your mind. This is your brand; it informs how you want to be and be seen.[11]

By going through this short process, you are underscoring what's most important to you and stripping away what's less important. None of us can be all things to all people. We admire people who are comfortable in their own skins—who know who they are. By narrowing those values down to a brand, you are ensuring that you project light that others can see. This is something you can use to make decisions, and even to weave into your discussions with other people.

Your personal presence brand is your anchor. It's a reminder in times of stress, distraction, tedium, or frustration what you want to show up to be and stand for. Most important, it's succinct and memorable enough to be called to mind whenever and wherever you need it.

For example, my top five values are Trustworthy, Generous, Creative, Inspiring, and Wholehearted. My brand is: "Open Mind, Brave Heart." It informs how I want to be in the world, as a parent and family member, in my work as a coach, and in my community. Also, it's important to note that these values are aspirational—how I want to be rather than how I am 100 percent of the time. Sure, I miss the mark sometimes, as my family would readily point out! But my brand keeps me in check and anchors me to what's important in times of stress or indecision. These important values serve as a compass for my behavior and how I communicate with others. When I'm in front of a room full of strangers or being tested with a tough client situation, I can take a moment, call my brand to mind and orient myself in the direction of my own values. Believe me, I use it.

If you'd like to do this on your own, follow those three steps. (For a little support, you can download a free tool at thehedgescompany .com.)

EMBRACE YOUR LEADERSHIP STORY

In Chapter 3, I discussed the downside of what happens when we buy into our own stories. Now I'm going to expand that concept, because there is a time when embracing our stories does help us to connect us with others. I call this your leadership story. It's a way of bringing your life experiences together in a cogent narrative. Your leadership story reveals enough of yourself so that others can get to know you and see what your values are.

Your leadership story tells people what you're all about.

Your leadership story doesn't have to be one specific story. Usually it's more of a compilation with an overall theme. Imagine this as a series of short stories in a volume named "Trust" or "Risk-Taking." Earlier, when I wrote about political candidates connecting with voters, this is what they're doing—revealing their back stories so that voters can understand them on a deeper level.

You see other well-respected leaders doing this with great impact. Howard Schultz, CEO of Starbucks, often talks about his early years growing up poor in public housing, and the impact that playing sports at the Boys and Girls Club had on him. This type of community support helped him to excel at sports and eventually attend college on an athletic scholarship. Starbucks, with its strong commitment to supporting local communities and causes, was among the first U.S. retailers to provide health insurance even to part-time workers. Schultz's story enables people to understand him as something more than another successful billionaire. It reveals his brand.

For a variety of reasons, leaders might not share their brand stories. Maybe they're embarrassed, or they feel it represents them in a bad light. They may believe that no one really cares. Remember that you get to write the narrative. Growing up poor could be something to hide, or like Shultz, something that creates a strong work ethic and sense of corporate responsibility. For now, I encourage you to reflect and embrace what has shaped your thinking and behavior to this point. We'll come back in a bit to discuss how to externalize it. (See Chapter 8 for how to structure a strong story).

OWN THE MESSAGE

A frequent frustration is how to convey and inspire with a message when it isn't your idea, and when you might not even agree with it. For example, you're a middle manager who has to rally your team around a new corporate vision that was handed down to you. If you've been in this situation, you know all too well how difficult it can be to find your game face.

There's always the option to undermine the message by telling others that it's "not what I would have done, but here you go." This kind of passive-aggressive, sabotaging behavior happens in companies every day. It kills change initiatives slowly but definitively. We're about inspiring here, and that's communicating to move in a positive direction.

At my firm, we call this "leadership maturity." It's the idea that when you take the job, you assume ownership over the messages and work product. It's your responsibility to dig into the message and determine how to make it your own. This may mean emphasizing the parts you do agree with, putting your own spin on it, showing the bright side of the change, or devising the way forward. It's finding the nugget inside of any message that aligns with your brand and goals. (If you can't do this with any degree of authenticity, you're probably in the wrong place.)

Leadership maturity is the idea that when you take the job, you assume ownership over the messages and make them your own.

Most important, it's not parroting talking points, but revealing your values *through* them. Others can only believe what they see that you believe. Whether you are conveying a product, an idea, or a mindset change, others need to see that it's clear to you.

AUTHENTICITY EXTERNALIZED

So now that we have some awareness around how to get clearer about the internal piece, it's time to express yourself in a way that allows others to see your good intentions. It can be maddeningly frustrating if, as was the case with Gabe, others misread your motives. It's even worse when they assume the negative.

While it's true that you can never please everyone, and you shouldn't expect to, it's to your advantage in Inspire Path conversations to present yourself honestly and authentically. Generally, when we do that, others reply in kind. Wharton professor Adam Grant's book *Give and Take* makes a compelling argument, backed by considerable research, that people tend to match each other's behaviors. When someone reveals something personal to us, we seek to return that favor.[12] We both learn more and try to understand each other's perspectives, and the relationship is enhanced. (We're also more likely to reach a mutually satisfactory outcome in negotiations.)

EXPLICIT TRANSPARENCY

We have an interesting relationship with transparency. For starters, we fear it. We spend a good deal of psychic effort trying to show our best selves.

Yet, we also believe that we, personally, are straightforward and readable most of the time. Recall what psychologists term *the transparency illusion*. We think that we're easy to read, but we're not. While strong emotions such as anger are readily detectable, subtle emotions are not.[13] Most of the time our emotions are subtle and controlled, and therefore hard to get across with accuracy. This is why you can have a two-hour conversation with someone and walk away with entirely different opinions of how the meeting went.

Most people think they are transparent but in fact, we're all very difficult to read.

To overcome this, we need to be explicitly transparent. This means not leaving it to chance, but putting our intention out there. One of the easiest ways to do this is by stating it up front, as discussed in Chapter 2. A simple, "here's my intention for this conversation" can change the direction entirely. Another way to be more transparent is to expose your thinking. With Inspire Path conversations, this may mean revealing the capitulations, concerns, and motives that led you to this place. When we practice explicit transparency, we never assume that others get where we're coming from. We tell them.

GENUINE LANGUAGE

How we speak also communicates our authenticity. We know that when someone uses stiff corporate-speak we're not going to connect. When we want to externalize our authenticity, we should sound like we do in any other part of our lives—using direct plain-speak that conveys our thoughts efficiently. While it's good to be thoughtful and to consider how we'll communicate, once we open our mouths, it's less about the exact wording than it is about the sentiment behind those words. Are we seen as genuine or as trying to impress? Are we more concerned with the connection we make or with the image we project?

We're more authentic when we sound like we do in any other part of our lives—using direct plain-speak that conveys our thoughts efficiently.

Another way that we can use language in a genuine way is to be brave enough to admit when we don't know something. Saying "I don't know" reveals that we're fallible and increases trust in us. Remember the pratfall effect: when we expose a weakness then our likeability goes up. It's the same idea here. Think of how much effort goes into trying to have every answer, from the time you're in school and want to please the teacher to last week when you wanted to please your boss. Being brave enough to be honest about what we do and do not know can be a true connection point.

VULNERABILITY EXPRESSED

I've touched upon vulnerability in this chapter quite a bit because authenticity requires a core of vulnerability. We know that no one is perfect or without weakness, so we feel safest and most honest when we see vulnerability expressed by others. We see it in ourselves all too well and are relieved to see it in others. This is not to say you should be a puddle of mush, or bring your darkest secrets to work, but reveal yourself to be a real person who has strengths and challenges like everyone else.

We feel safest and most honest when we see vulnerability expressed by others.

So how do you express the kind of vulnerability that makes those connections? First, make sure that you know and share your leadership story. Whenever possible, weave those vignettes into your conversations so the other party can better get you on a basic human level.

Second, strive to be real. Do not try to convey an overly positive version of yourself. One of my favorite quotes around this is from the movie *Almost Famous*. In the scene, Philip Seymour Hoffman plays a grizzled journalist who is helping a young protégé figure out the ways of the world. Hoffman's character encourages him not to be ashamed of being real by telling him that the only real exchanges in the world come when we're being uncool. Indeed, you could argue that connection doesn't really start until we know we're dealing with the real person across the table.

Finally, another way that we can express vulnerability is to ask for advice. You can ask anyone, up or down the hierarchy, in a position of power or not. Seeking advice is a powerful method of connecting. Research at Northwestern has shown that when we ask another person for advice we enhance the relationship on multiple levels.[14] We show competence without sacrificing warmth. We help others to take our perspective, which creates more mutually desirable outcomes. And we inspire increased commitment. There is one catch: The advice has to be sincerely sought. No asking just for the sake of asking.

Let that settle in. We generate trust and competence just by asking for another person's advice. Yet, how often do we try to avoid asking in order to figure something out on our own? When we ask for advice we are gaining buy-in and commitment for our ideas—not by telling, but by asking.

AUTHENTICITY GIVEN
INVITES AUTHENTICITY RECEIVED

In conversations that matter, all parties need to open up. This is an inherent risk, but if we don't manage this, the communication is nothing more than ricocheting ideas off each other. Nothing actually gets through.

As the leader, authenticity begins with you. It has to be modeled. It's not enough to feel like you're authentic; you also must actively show it. Gabe, from earlier in this chapter, used the various aspects of this framework to allow others to better understand his intentions, so they could begin to feel secure with his leadership. He didn't understand why he'd need to do this at first. After all, this had never been a problem and he knew what he was trying to get across. But his authenticity didn't scale. It was only through first getting clear about his own values and leadership story, and then consciously and purposefully choosing to be transparent in interpersonal as well as in group interactions that he was able to change that impression. He was successful, though it took the good part of a year of consistently working on relationships throughout the company. As our work wrapped, he was being groomed for a position on the executive team.

We can role model authenticity on even the largest scales. Indra Nooyi, the CEO of PepsiCo, is one of the most highly regarded leaders in the Fortune 500. Named the fifteenth most powerful woman in the world by Forbes, she took the helm of the company in 2006, and began a global transformation effort to change the business structure and culture.[15] Nooyi is generous with her leadership story. A deep believer in an authentic approach, she speaks publicly about the secret to her success being a culture where people could be "wholehearted" at work and bring the entirety of themselves to their jobs every day.[16]

Perhaps the best that any of us can wish for is not to *be* authentic but to live authentically—to choose to show up as our true selves and connect on a real level as a default posture. Bill George uses a metaphor for authenticity that's apt. He says to "think of your life as a house, with a bedroom for your personal life, a study for your professional life, a family room for your family, and a living room to share with friends. Can you knock down the walls between these rooms and be the same person in each of them?"[17]

That's the person we're most inspired by.

TAKEAWAYS

FROM CHAPTER 4

◎ We're most inspiring when we're authentic, yet authenticity is a struggle for many people in the workplace who have been trained to display an unflappable, impassive, calm demeanor.

◎ We admire people who speak the truth, talk directly, and show their convictions. This is apparent in the leaders we admire and in the popularity of TED Talks.

◎ Though counterintuitive, showing authenticity is something we can work on. We're adaptively authentic, where we learn new behaviors and integrate them into our own way of being.

◎ Authentic communicators should blend a mix of competency with vulnerability. These two dimensions, exhibited together, have been shown to connect others to us.

◎ To be a more authentic leader, work on authenticity internalized and externalized. Internalized authenticity means knowing our core values and brand, having a cogent leadership story, and owning the messages we communicate. Externalized authenticity means being explicitly transparent, using genuine language, and expressing vulnerability.

CHAPTER 5

LIFTING SIGHTS TOWARD POTENTIAL

"I see greatness in you."

Let's say that you walk into work tomorrow, like any other day, with a project or a particular issue on your mind. But after you settle into your desk, someone you respect takes you aside, makes you feel as if you are the most important item of the day, and speaks sincerely about your potential. What if this person were also your boss? How might you feel about yourself and your ability to succeed? Would your confidence grow? How about your loyalty?

If a boss, colleague, coach, relative, or friend has reached out in such a way, I bet you recall that conversation and replay it from time to time. It may have changed what you thought was possible for yourself. It informed your choices or decisions, and what risks you felt equipped to take. When we've been lucky enough to have these conversations in our own lives—when someone has shined a light on our own potential—then that illustrates how meaningful that person is in a personal way.

Recognizing another's potential—sincerely, specifically, and altruistically—is one of the most powerful and inspiring conversations we can have. Certainly these exchanges play a large role in inspirational leadership in general. As such, they can be part of a larger Inspire Path conversation. To clarify, conveying potential is not about pumping someone up to get that person to do something. It's not about manipulating or pandering. We do not share this to get anything in return, though we often are rewarded with loyalty and commitment. Conversations about potential have the impact they do because we offer them with Chapter 3's NATO—no attachment to the outcome *for us*. We simply want to benefit the other person.

Recognizing another's potential—sincerely, specifically, and altruistically—is one of the most powerful and inspiring conversations we can have.

We know that feedback is important to growth in any setting, especially at work. But conversations about potential aren't the same as positive feedback, though there can be an overlap. Positive feedback— which is provided to encourage certain behavior—is given around a particular work area or function. Conversations about potential are primarily about the person, not the job—and they aren't directive. We're putting our thoughts out there, and the other person can choose what to do with them.

At their core, potential conversations are about what's possible. They lift people's heads out of their day-to-day routine to see something larger in themselves. They allow people to connect dots and recognize themes. They are a pure form of connection. They honor someone else by acknowledging what you see within that person.

Potential conversations are about what's possible.

A conversation about potential:

- Acknowledges someone's strengths
- Shows people what they're capable of
- Honors a success
- Helps people see what you believe is possible for them from your vantage point

Conversations about potential can exist one-to-one or one-to-many. A good organizational vision communicates potential. Visions lift organizations up and show them what's possible. They encourage the collective to see an organization's strengths and greatness. Visions tell us that we can achieve more because we're capable of being more.

Consider these examples of potential-oriented visions. The airline JetBlue's vision is "Inspiring Humanity." It states, "In the air and on the ground, we're committed to bettering the lives of our customers, crewmembers, and communities—and inspiring others to do the same."[1] Bettering lives is a lofty vision for a for-profit corporation. It takes people out of their day-to-day functional jobs and orients them toward a larger purpose. In 2012, Volvo made a groundbreaking vision statement with a literally lifesaving purpose: to have zero deaths in its automobiles by 2020.[2] It was bold, risky, and meaningful. You can imagine how coalescing that kind of vision can be as traffic accidents have the potential to affect everyone, including every employee at Volvo.

But visions that communicate potential don't need to be as grand. Ford Motor Company united behind "One Ford" to become the automotive powerhouse it is today. That may not sound all that inspiring at first. But remember, in 2008 the carmaker faced the worst-ever financial loss in its 105-year history, and was plagued by divisional infighting, falling sales, and a lackluster product line. Then-CEO Alan Mulally realized this vision by bringing Ford back as "One Ford," ultimately becoming one of the most successful and admired car companies in the world.[3]

These are visions on a corporate scale, but visions also exist on an individual scale. We have visions for ourselves. As you no doubt know from times when someone has called out your potential, these conversations don't have to be lengthy or even involved. A quick, off-the-cuff exchange can be resonant and meaningful. In my own life, most of them were exactly that: someone took me aside for a brief moment to spotlight something positive about me. Short, sweet, and very, very powerful.

SO WHAT'S SO POWERFUL ABOUT SEEING POTENTIAL?

In the mid-1960s, a psychologist named Robert Rosenthal and an elementary school principal named Lenore Jacobson got together to research a curious question: What impact do teacher expectations have on student performance? They decided to conduct a study of California elementary school students to find out. At the beginning of the school year, they had students take an IQ test but kept the results secret. Then they told the teachers that some students (regardless of actual IQ) were "intellectual bloomers" and thus, were academically superior to their classmates. The teachers spent the school year teaching all of the students in a routine classroom setting. At the end of the study, the researchers had all the students retake the same IQ test. They found that these faux "intellectual bloomers" scored significantly higher on the retake than their peers—regardless of their actual IQ at the start. It turns out that students will rise or fall based on the expectations that authority figures have of them.[4] The researchers called this the *Pygmalion effect.*

That was fifty years ago, and surely things have changed, right? Actually, this phenomenon has been replicated by research many times over in the years since.[5] The Pygmalion effect's ramifications go far beyond academic settings. How people in authority view us becomes a self-fulfilling prophecy: We rise or fall to their expectations. The cause is twofold. First, the authority figure treats us differently in subtle and unsubtle ways—perhaps giving us special attention and communicating with us like we're smart—which changes how we think and behave. Second, when we learn that we are thought of highly, we change our behavior to meet that expectation.

A bevy of research in management has emerged based on this principle, across industries and fields.[6] All leaders, whether in the classroom or the boardroom, have tremendous power simply by being in positions of authority. They possess the ability to influence how others view themselves. When you call out people's greatness, the recipients see the greatness too.

Leaders, through their positions of authority, have tremendous power to influence how others view themselves.

Communicating potential is also meaningful because it reminds us of our strengths. Gallup conducted a voluminous amount of research around the impact of using our strengths at work. According to the findings, when people use their strengths at work, doing what they do best every day, they are six times as likely to be engaged and three times as likely to say they have an excellent quality of life.[7] This makes sense. When we tap into our strengths we are using our innate talents, and that feels fun and rewarding. If you've ever been in a position of not using your strengths every day (which Gallup says is the situation with half of Americans) then you know what drudgery work can be.

Communicating potential helps people access their strengths.

Luckily, for many people with professional jobs, there are ways to incorporate your strengths into your work. When we identify another's potential, we are generally in a discussion around strengths. We are highlighting an inherent talent that can be featured and grown. It's so easy to forget what our strengths are—assuming we ever really knew—that having someone we respect validate our strengths is inspirational. I remember taking a strengths-assessment in the midst of building my last company. The results said that my top strength was creativity. I thought I had filled out the test wrong! It took a trusted colleague to help me recognize my own creative strength. (And here I am today writing books.)

Finally, when we highlight potential, we boost confidence. Confidence has an oversized impact on our effectiveness, and yet, we can't just turn it on like a switch. (The more we try, the more it backfires.) When someone we respect—and who may even be in a position of authority—tells us what she believes we can do, we will borrow that person's confidence in us. We may not have all the confidence required, but it only takes a little to begin tackling the challenges that will allow our own confidence to grow.

When we highlight potential, we boost confidence.

When I first contemplated becoming an entrepreneur, I was twenty-eight and had no idea how to run a company. At that point, I had a whopping four years of professional experience after graduate school. I might have easily been talked out of it. But then I told a colleague whom I admired and valued what I was considering. He told me that I *had* to do it. He said that I possessed an unusual ability to figure things out for myself, and that he thought I would figure this out too. I'd never identified that quality in myself, and his belief in me spoke volumes. It allowed me to see myself as he saw me. His insights fortified me.

This is the reason that pointing out potential can be so meaningful. When we take the time to do it, we are helping to create a virtuous cycle where people can do more, because they believe they can. In my experience, most people don't have conversations about potential because they're not thinking about it. With so many urgent conversations having to happen, a meandering compliment session may seem irrelevant or over the top. As a younger manager, it wouldn't have dawned on me to do this, I'll admit. But today I'm a much different leader and person. We have the power to unlock the potential in others; we simply have to think about it—whether friend-to-friend, colleague-to-colleague, or boss-to-employee.

SUPERBOSSES AND SUPER POTENTIAL

Anyone can call out someone's potential, and it can be inspiring. I bet if a near-stranger came up to you after seeing you talk at a meeting and praised your strengths, you'd be affected. You'd certainly get a little skip in your step (assuming the person wasn't creepy, of course).

But as the Pygmalion effect shows us, when we combine authority with recognizing potential, then we get something even more powerful. Leaders who focus on potential are the ones people clamor to work for. They create the visionary organizations that possess an energetic momentum.

In his book, *Superbosses: How Exceptional Leaders Master the Flow of Talent*, Dartmouth Management Professor Sydney Finkelstein examines how exceptional leaders cultivate talent.[8] Finkelstein set out to understand a pattern: In any given industry, many of the top leaders have at one time worked for the same person. These "superbosses" are preternaturally able to hone and develop talent that spreads throughout the industry and establishes new successful ventures. He cites leaders such as Ralph Lauren, Mary Kay Ash, George Lucas, and Lorne

Michaels, as well as several less widely known leaders who are none-theless famous in their industries.

Superbosses instill a sense of confidence in their people, and highlight their exceptionalism.

In more than two hundred interviews, Finkelstein found that super-bosses hired talented people, but that was just the beginning. They also worked hands-on with their employees to help them accomplish things even larger than what the employees believed was possible. The super-bosses communicated high expectations, and they certainly demanded a lot. But they also built up their teams by instilling "a sense of confidence and exceptionalism" in their people, who then rose to the challenge and beyond. Superbosses stayed connected with their people, helping them long after they left the company. For example, Lorne Michaels has pro-duced dozens of shows for ex-*Saturday Night Live* cast members. The relationships clearly matter to superbosses, who become lifelong mentors and collaborators, helping to sow potential indefinitely.

Finkelstein described it to me this way: "Superbosses recognize po-tential. Many people I interviewed said that the leader saw something in them that they didn't even know they had. I heard a story the other day of an executive who, when twenty-eight, was sent to Japan by his boss. He told his boss, 'I'm not ready.' The boss told him, 'I'll give you a safety net a couple of times, and I know you can do it or I wouldn't ask you.' He did it, and was successful, and looks back on it as a water-shed moment."

"When you have a boss who encourages your potential, and then you successfully conquer a big challenge, you feel as if there's nothing you can't do. It really is a career accelerator. Superbosses know this and foster it. Their default is to create opportunities."[9]

In a similar vein, former Oracle executive Liz Wiseman's book *Mul-tipliers: How the Best Leaders Make Everyone Smarter* explores how certain leaders get so much from their people while others don't.[10] In her research, she discovered that leaders can be categorized as *multipliers*, who increase the intelligence of their teams, and *diminishers*, who underutilize their people and stifle creativity. Lots of us have worked with diminishers—micromanagers and generally bad bosses who leave us feeling drained. On the other hand, multipliers, Wiseman found, acknowledge a person's "native genius"—not just what she does well, but also what she loves to do. Multipliers make smart people smarter, and ignite their strengths. They see and multiply potential.

Similar to superbosses, multipliers see and multiply potential. They ignite strengths.

It's not an accident—multipliers make the effort. In an interview for the book, Wiseman explained it this way: "It struck me how deliberate multipliers are about how they lead. They had a meta process for management, or a cognition of why it's a good approach. They weren't just doing the work of leading, but were deliberate about their own approach to leadership. There wasn't a single pattern for the leaders—some were more demanding, and others were more nurturing. But there was a planned and considered approach to how they worked."[11]

You may think that you have to be a name-brand leader or run a Fortune 500 company to be a multiplier or a superboss. Not at all. Organizations of all sizes and bents have leaders who invest in their people's potential. I don't run across them every day, but I do find them, and occasionally I'm lucky enough to work with them.

At the beginning of any coaching engagement, I put together a leadership assessment by speaking to numerous people who work with my client. The interviewees can be direct reports, board members, peers, or employees several levels down the chain. I'm looking to get an accurate picture of how my client shows up in a work setting, including strengths and areas for development. I'm also learning about the client's presence, management approach, reputation, and leadership impact.

Asking people to give feedback on someone who may be their boss or even their boss's boss can be a sensitive conversation. I'm always impressed by the candor that people bring to these discussions. The interviewees tell me a lot. Sometimes it seems they've been waiting for years for me to call and ask them! Most of the time, the feedback is fairly evenhanded—some positive, some critical—and in a professional tone that's typical in a work environment.

But every once in a while I get a different reaction. Instead of listing the client's strengths and weaknesses, the conversation will be dominated by what my client has done for the interviewee. More than providing feedback, the interviewee wants to acknowledge and thank the person. I recall one such interview process that blew me away. The feedback was about a client who had built a rapidly growing company. People were catching their breath from the change. Now, you might think you'd hear critiques about the leader being a hard driver. (I sure expected to.) Instead, I was regaled with tales of what a role model the leader was, and how people wanted to work harder for him. They talked about his integrity and values, and how he brought out the best in his people. A few participants actually said they loved him as a person, and compared the company to a family. Every single interviewee said he was the best boss they'd ever had.

Uh huh, I thought, I found one. Superboss. Multiplier. Potential communicator. Inspirer.

CONCEPT IN ACTION

TO RECOGNIZE POTENTIAL:
PUT THESE WORDS IN YOUR MOUTH

Calling out potential in others may feel somewhat foreign because many of us simply don't do it. Hopefully (hint, hint) we have these conversations with our children and our loved ones and can consider how we've approached those. It can be awkward if you're not already wired to talk this way. If you're worried about coming across as over-the-top or insincere, don't be. Sharing potential can be a quick conversation, as I mentioned above. It need only be authentic and delivered without expectation. We can weave these conversations easily into the daily course of our work and lives. We think these thoughts already; it's only a matter of spitting them out.

Here are five straightforward ways to communicate potential in those around you. Of course there's an unlimited number of ways to have these conversations, and I'm certainly not trying to suggest there's a right or a wrong way to do it. Rather, I'm hoping to point out that getting these conversations started is not very difficult or formal. And frankly, sometimes the conversation only needs to be one comment sincerely given, either alone or in the middle of a larger Inspire Path conversation.

Conversations about potential don't need to be formal, and can even be one comment sincerely given.

TO COMMUNICATE POTENTIAL IN OTHERS, SAY:
"I see _____ in you."
"You're always good at _____."
"I'm proud of you for _____."
"I've seen how you've grown/progressed."
"Let me share what I see is possible for you."
"What would you do if anything were possible?"

"I see _____ in you."

Perhaps the simplest way to recognize potential in another person is to just say what you see in that person. It may be greatness, skillfulness, kindness, effectiveness, leadership, or a spot-on sense of humor. The list goes on. By stating what we see, we are externalizing what we're already thinking. And remember, we all have those innate strengths that are too often forgotten. By drawing attention to them, we're validating what makes another person exceptional to us.

Even better, there's no way for the other person to reject this comment. It's your perspective, plain and simple. You're just putting it out there.

"You're always good at _____."

Most leaders do provide positive feedback to their teams, though not as often as they should. In general, this is around a point in time or a specific event. For example, "You ran that product launch very well." Rarely do we elevate this conversation to underscore what talent is allowing the person to be successful. And potential feedback isn't about behavior change; it's offered as a gift with no attachments.

This type of conversation about potential helps people home in on what they consistently do well. That knowledge can take them into the realm of what's possible. Let's say a product manager is effective because she's able to bring people together behind a common goal. She's a mobilizer. Calling attention to this competency allows her to see her own contribution in a much broader way. If a leader tells her that then she can seek out opportunities to continue exploring those strengths, even if it means stretching out of product management to try new avenues.

"I'm proud of you for _____."

This statement may feel a little off to some of you, and I understand why. Outside of our children and other close loved ones, we don't often tell other people that we're proud of them. There's even an implied hierarchical line that may feel iffy to cross: It's okay to tell people below us that we're proud of them, but not anyone else. (No matter how senior someone is to you, however, I've found everyone appreciates hearing "I'm proud to work for you" or "I'm proud to work with you.")

However, all of that is precisely why expressing pride can be meaningful and inspiring to another person. We don't hear it very much. And when it's offered with sincerity, communicating pride brings a sort of humanity to the conversation that stands out. It says, "I'm invested in you" in a deep way.

"I've observed how you've grown/progressed."

In the forward momentum of our lives, we rarely look back to appreciate the hard work and growth we've achieved. That's a shame, because seeing that progress teaches us about our abilities, strengths, and potential. When we call this out for another, we're creating a space to honor that person's journey. We're pausing to bring color to the history a person has zipped through.

By offering this observation, we're helping someone take ownership and value development and potential. It also shows that you've been bearing witness to another person's path, which communicates investment.

"Let me share what I see is possible for you."

This is about creating a vision. It works as well for a person as for an entire organization. It's painting a picture of a future that the other person might not even know is possible. Storytelling can be particularly effective here, as a way to help the other person step inside of this vision and try it on for size. Again, it's up to the others to do what they want to do with it. This conversation about possibility enlarges the other person's perspective and shows what could be.

It's probably obvious to you why this can be so inspiring: You invite the person to imagine an expanded reality. When we see the future for ourselves, all the baggage of our doubts, fears, and practicalities handcuffs it. When others share their vision for us, it's not dragged down by any of that; it's pure possibility. I've seen well-put conversations like this change lives almost overnight—moving someone from a place of stasis to a newly defined future.

"What would you do if anything were possible?

This powerful question is a different approach than the previous suggestions. We can tell people the potential we see, and we can also guide them to discover it on their own. As was just discussed, we approach our future handcuffed and limited. Fear is the heavy foot putting the brakes on our aspirations.

This question forces the other person to put aside his fear and engage in his own untethered vision. It doesn't deny the fear; it sidesteps it. And when we can help another person think through his potential unrestricted, he can begin to separate possibilities from fear. Having used this question often in coaching, I've observed that more often than not, other people end up disavowing some of the fear that had been holding them back. By sampling the potential—turning it around in their minds and making it real—they are often willing to invest in themselves in newly committed ways.

POTENTIAL BOOSTS ON THE INSPIRE PATH

So now you have some "easy ins" to insert more conversations about potential into your world. You can make communicating potential part of any conversation where you want to connect and inspire. It may be part of a larger way that you want to show up as a leader, colleague, or friend. No matter, it's a gift that requires little from you, but offers much to the recipient. As with any inspiring conversation, you never know where the impact ends. When our potential is called out and acknowledged, we tuck away the moment and pull it out when we need it—even decades later.

When we choose to externalize the possibilities that we see for others, we also change how they view themselves. We enlarge and expand perspective. We encourage and build confidence. Very often, we also make someone's day. Pretty awesome result for saying what we already think.

TAKEAWAYS

FROM CHAPTER 5

- ◉ The simple act of outwardly recognizing another person's potential—sincerely and altruistically—is one of the most powerful and inspiring conversations we can have.

- ◉ Inspiring corporate visions are conversations about potential on a large scale. They tell the organization that it can achieve more because it's capable of being more.

- ◉ Conversations about potential invoke the "Pygmalion effect." Research shows that people rise or fall to the expectations of those in authority. In other words, it's a self-fulfilling prophecy.

- ◉ Conversations about potential are also affecting because they remind us of our innate strengths, which are easily overlooked or forgotten. Acknowledgment also builds confidence.

- ◉ Conversations about potential need not be formal or lengthy. The most impactful ones are often extemporaneous and in the moment. A simple "I see this is in you" or "I'm proud of you" can have far-reaching meaning for another.

CHAPTER 6

THE QUIET INFLUENCE OF LISTENING

A s I mentioned in the introduction, the Harris Poll research I commissioned found that listening was the most-cited communication behavior of inspirational people. More than half of respondents stated that listening was the most inspiring communication behavior they've experienced. Listening is part of this section on being personal because when we're listened to it feels as though someone is personally investing in us. It signals commitment. Yet, here's the paradox: Think of how much more time and energy we put into how we transmit information than how we take it in. There's no comparison. In large part, that's because we already believe we're good listeners.

That was certainly the case with me. After deciding to shift my career into leadership coaching about a decade ago, I attended Georgetown University's certification program. I felt pretty confident going in, figuring it would be worth the time and effort if I personally enjoyed it and fine-tuned a few skills in the process. Just a few hours into the six-month-long program, I was duly humbled. There was a tremendous amount about coaching that I didn't know. One of my most surprising realizations was that I needed to learn how to listen.

Now, at that point in my career, I had built a business where I prided myself on truly listening and understanding customers. I had managed a talented team of people. Not to mention, I'd spent my career as a communications professional!

And yet, I had a long way to go before I could listen deeply and intuitively, the way that coaches need to with clients. I vividly remember roleplaying with other coaches to practice deep listening, and becoming exhausted.

Having to pay this much attention was clearly something I needed to build muscle around. And so I did—but only after I shifted ingrained habits and spent many months practicing new behaviors. Today I can go into deep listening mode when needed. While not everyone needs to listen like a coach, the methodologies are useful for anyone. After reading this chapter, my hope is that you'll be able to deepen your listening in ways that inspire others.

Listening as a skill comes up throughout our business and personal lives. Listening signals respect. It shows that we value the speaker. We desperately want our leaders and our teams to listen to us. When we're in the decisionmaking spot, we are often bombarded with differing viewpoints that require us to listen thoroughly so that we can make the best call. Our customers want to be heard and validated. Our closest friends and family ask for us to listen, and call us out when we don't.

Psychologist Mark Goulston, author of *Just Listen*, believes that listening is a primary way of showing others what they're worth to us. He writes, "It's not good enough for us to know in our own hearts that we're valuable; we need to see our worth reflected in the eyes of the people around us."[1]

In Inspire Path conversations, attentive listening plays an important role. When people describe inspirational figures in their lives, they say the person made them feel truly listened to—almost as if time stopped for their conversation. Listening at that level conveys an emotional and personal investment. It says: Your opinion is so valuable that I'm going to devote myself not just to hearing you, but to fully understanding you as well.

Deep listening conveys an emotional and personal investment.

Deep listening takes more than catching someone else's words. It can be exhausting, and just plain hard. That's because in any conversation there's a whole lot more going on than two people taking turns speaking. To truly listen, you first must be attuned to the larger dynamics at play.

TALK IS CHEAP, LISTENING IS EXPENSIVE

On the surface, a conversation seems straightforward. You talk, I listen. I talk, you listen. We each understand what the other is trying to convey. If only it were that easy there would be no need to write about it. But we know that miscommunications abound. And one of the primary reasons is because in any single conversation there are actually multiple conversations. There's what you're saying and I'm saying *and* what we're each saying to ourselves. Figure 6.1 illustrates this concept.

In any single conversation there are actually multiple conversations.

Think about it. Every time you open your mouth, there's a running narrative also going in your head. It starts before you utter your first word, and it runs the entire time you're talking. Interestingly, if we don't actively manage it, we pay *more* attention to our internal conversation than to the one we're having externally. You notice this in yourself when you miss entire parts of a conversation lost in your own thoughts.

Figure 6.1: Two Separate Conversations at Play

As the graphic illustrates, the words we say and the thoughts we engage in don't even have to match. In fact, they usually don't. At best, we speak a subset of the thoughts we're having. Generally, this is a good thing. Learning to self-censor is an important part of emotional intelligence. However, this thinking/speaking dichotomy gets in the way of listening. It's practically impossible to pay rapt attention to two conversations at once—especially when they aren't even the same conversations at their core. You can see that there's an entirely different conversation happening internally than the words these two talking heads are vocalizing. (This would certainly exacerbate the issues around deliverables.)

It's nearly impossible to pay rapt attention to two conversations at once—and even harder when they're two different ones.

Professor Ralph Nichols, considered the "father of the field of listening," was one of the research pioneers who addressed the impact of our thoughts on listening. Nichols spent forty years studying how people listen and how to improve listening skills. Through his research at the University of Wisconsin, Nichols found that, on the whole, we are very poor listeners.[2] Among the findings in his research published with colleague Leonard A. Stevens: After listening to someone speak in a public setting, the average person only remembers 50 percent of what was just heard—regardless of how accurately and carefully the person was trying to listen. After two months, people lose 75 percent of what was said. Keep going and it's practically as if the conversation never happened.

Research has shown that we retain only 50 percent of what a person has just said, no matter how hard we try to listen.

Nichols identified one of the root causes of our poor listening: the gap between the speed of our words and the pace of our thoughts. The average rate of speech for Americans is 125 words per minute, while our thoughts race considerably faster. To truly listen we actually have to slow down our processing to be attentive to the other person. But that's not what we usually do. We fill that attention gap by using our minds in other ways, such as evaluating the situation, trying to jump ahead and solve the problem, comparing what they're saying with our own experience, or taking mental sidetracks that are unrelated to the conversation at hand.

We've all been in conversations where we're speaking and we can see that we've lost the other person for a few seconds. Nichols and Stevens argue that we misuse this "spare thinking time." We divert our attention from the conversation when we should be "listening between the lines"—in other words using the opportunity to hunt for meaning.

We can do this by paying attention to speakers' nonverbal cues and tone, mentally noting their key points, and trying to get to the true heart of the conversation. In other words, by looking beneath the words to the discussion's actual subtext.

THE SUBTEXT IS SCREAMING
IF YOU LISTEN FOR IT

Just as in any conversation there's an external and an internal dialogue, there's also a text and a subtext. The text is the words that we're speaking. The subtext is the underlying meaning. It's the context of the conversation—our thoughts, history, past interactions, emotions, larger culture, and expectations. When we attempt to listen, we generally focus on the words—or the text. And yes, that's better than letting our thoughts wander to our errand lists. But all too often we miss the subtext, which gives us a much fuller picture of the situation before us.

Unless we listen for it, probe to understand it and deliberately bring it into the conversation, the subtext sits untouched. It's the elephant in the room that both parties either ignore or don't see at all. But it has an oversized bearing on our understanding.

Unless we listen for it, probe to understand it, and deliberately bring it into the conversation, the subtext sits there untouched.

In Figure 6.1, the text is focused on the deliverable. The subtext is that this is a strained relationship where neither the manager's nor the worker's needs are being met. If we were to creatively extrapolate this example, the subtext could also be a department that's understaffed, or a culture that can't communicate difficult conversations openly. When we include the subtext in our understanding by listening for it, and even probing to find it, then we learn far more than what the words convey.

A recurring situation in my work that demonstrates our failure to listen for and explore subtext involves employee feedback. Here's a typical scenario: A supervisor or HR leader reaches out to me about working with one of their executives, and I ask what the executive's development issues are for coaching. I hear a list of concerns, and then I ask, "How much have you shared with the executive?" The leader assures me that the executive has been well informed about both the issues and their criticality.

Then I speak to the executive, who tells me he's not exactly sure why he's been referred for coaching. He's been given some light feedback as part of an annual review, but he's not sure what he should work on, or if it's even a priority. He's open to coaching for his own development, yet he needs clarification on what he should change.

This scenario happens so frequently in coaching it's practically a cliché. If it occurred once or twice, you might assume that the person giving the feedback isn't a competent communicator. But it happens over and over again. Clearly something else is going on. This is the delivery of personal, career-impacting feedback. You'd think both parties would pay rapt attention throughout the entire conversation. Yet, two people walk away having dramatically differing views of what just transpired. What gives?

Commonly, two people walk away from a conversation with dramatically different ideas of what just transpired.

Below I've sketched out an example lining up the text and subtexts to show what's really happening in these feedback conversations.

TEXT (WHAT WAS SAID)	SUBTEXT (WHAT WASN'T SAID)
Sarah (Brad's boss): Brad, do you have a minute? I want to run something by you.	Sarah's trying to strike a casual touch so as not to alarm Brad about this feedback. He can be defensive so she wants to gently toss it out there.
Brad: Sure, Sarah. Do you want to talk now or should we schedule a time?	Brad tries to figure out how important this issue is. Does it require a dedicated hour on the calendar? He's trying to finish an important proposal.
Sarah: Now's good. This won't take long. I wanted to discuss some feedback I've received from your peers. You're hitting all of your metrics, and you know I think you're a tremendous asset here. But there are some people who don't understand your style, and can take you the wrong way. I'd like you to work on building better relationships with your peers.	Sarah needs to keep Brad motivated. He's the company's top salesperson. She doesn't want to demoralize Brad so she leads with what he does well. In the past, he's gotten argumentative so she tries to let him know that everyone isn't out to get him. But the truth is, his peers think he's a bully.
Brad: I'm surprised to hear that. Just last week Greg asked for my help on a project, and I stayed late to give him advice. Jen is in my office every day bouncing ideas around with me. I pride myself on working with others.	Brad can't believe this! He feels he's the hardest worker on the team and goes out of his way to help people do their own jobs. He knows plenty about relationships—after all he's in sales. Frankly, Sarah is the one who isn't managing relationships well at her level. Brad's heard rumors that she's reached her limit at the company.
Sarah: Certainly you work well with some of your peers, and it's impossible to please everyone. But your go-getter style can ruffle feathers, especially with the more analytical types. It would help all of us if you could take a more collaborative approach.	Sarah tries to pump Brad's confidence by making it about a style mismatch. All he needs to do is be respectful to people, and she hopes he can do that. She'd be happy if her team just stopped complaining about him. She's got more important things to focus on.
Brad: I hear you. Collaboration is something everyone can work on, and that includes me. I'll focus on it.	Brad decides this isn't worth fighting over. He'll focus on his metrics, because that's what his bonus is based on. Sarah's boss just reached out to Brad to let him know what a great job he's doing in sales. Maybe it's because Sarah's on her way out? Looks like Brad's on track to beat the sales record this year.
Sarah: Thanks, Brad. I knew you would. Now let's talk about that new sales meeting you set up. Great job on that.	Sarah doesn't want to end this on a negative note so she veers into positive territory. She's glad he accepted the feedback and hopes this matter is settled.

As you can see, Sarah and Brad's verbal conversation is only a fraction of what's actually happening. In the text, Sarah is asking Brad to work on collaboration, and he agrees. But in the subtext, Sarah is trying to manage a disruptive bully on her team, placating him enough to change his behavior but keep him motivated on sales. On the other hand, Brad has evidence to suggest that Sarah's feedback isn't all that valid. You can imagine why Brad doesn't "hear" what Sarah is saying, and how they could leave that room with different ideas of what happened.

This idea of text and subtext doesn't just happen with challenging conversations—it happens with most conversations. That's why so many conversations miss the point, and why people don't feel heard. Listening only feels real when we speak about both the text and the subtext. That's why inspirational communication resonates so personally for us—another person identifies and listens to the full experience that we're having.

Ignoring the subtext is why so many conversations miss the point, and why people don't feel heard.

LISTENING TAKES MOST OF OUR TIME AND YET . . .

So listening is a critical skill with multiple moving parts that's difficult to get right. It's also rarely focused on as a professional competency. Let me guess that you've never been to a training session on listening skills. (If you have, congrats, you're in a minority.) If we ever learn communication skills, the emphasis is generally on *speaking*. We attend trainings for public speaking, get mentored on how to speak up in meetings, and take management courses on how to sell a message. It's as if our success and influence come from only what we say.

**We spend far more of our time listening than speaking, yet
we rarely get training on listening as a communication skill.**

There's an irony here since we spend far more of our time listening than speaking. Consider your average meeting or conference call. You devote most of the time to listening (or you are supposed to, anyway). Even if you're presenting in a meeting, there's likely just as much time allocated to questions and discussion where you'll also need to listen carefully.

Listening is a desired quality in others. Calling someone a "good listener" is high praise. In their work studying how listening skills shape perception in the workplace, research professors John Haas and Christa Arnold found that listening skills had a significant role in how we assess another's communication effectiveness.[3] According to their analysis, listening behaviors accounted for a full one-third of the characteristics that perceivers use to evaluate a coworker's overall communication competence. This supports my own experience that we're just as—or even more—likely to be impactful through our listening as through our speaking.

Some companies do tout a commitment to helping their leaders adopt stronger listening skills. General Electric Chairman and CEO Jeff Immelt said that "humble listening" was one of the top four characteristics in leaders.[4] When a leader points to listening as a core competency, that's a positive sign—and a timely one. With the complexity and speed of change in business, and frankly, our overall globally connected environments, we need people to be open and to listen.

As CEO of the Association for Talent Development Tony Bingham observes, "Technology breaks down the barriers of time and space, and that has contributed to an expectation of connection, accountability, and purpose. Social media has changed the landscape of how we communicate and what we expect from communication."[5]

With changing expectations of leaders being felt, every once in a while I'll see listening incorporated into leadership development or corporate training. The solutions provided are frequently a version of active listening, such as:

- **Paraphrasing**: "I hear you say that . . ."
- **Using I statements vs. You statements**: "I feel/believe/want . . ." vs. "You did . . ."
- **Owning Emotions**: "When you say that, I feel . . . "

These can be good tools to have on hand. There's certainly nothing wrong with this approach, yet many people feel contrived talking this way. And unfortunately, this type of active listening has made its way into popular culture in the form of parodies and late-night comedy spoofs. Further, when we are so intent on using a certain communication convention, it can take us out of the deep listening mode we're trying for in the first place.

Instead, I've found we can improve our listening more profoundly if we make a shift from *how* we're listening to *what* we're listening for. In other words, start listening like a coach.

CONCEPT IN ACTION

SHIFT YOUR LISTENING TO OPEN YOUR UNDERSTANDING

It may feel like overkill to learn to listen like a coach—after all, most of you aren't coaches and don't care to be. Yet, this type of listening can benefit anyone. If you know how to shift your listening, you can go into deep and inspirational listening mode whenever you choose to. You can also recognize when you're slipping away from it. And if you're having a meaningful conversation with someone, then you can identify where your listening needs to be.

> **If you know how to shift your listening, you can go into deep and inspirational listening mode whenever you choose to.**

I identify four key shifts in this section that you can make when you're trying to listen intently. They all require you to move from *how* you listen to *what* you're listening for. Rather than providing techniques, they offer you a way to listen naturally, so you can take in a fuller picture of information and gain a greater understanding.

Let's also be frank: This type of listening takes more time, and it requires a heavier emotional investment. You have to be prepared for that. Certainly not every conversation requires deep listening. Many are quick exchanges where we don't need to go much further than the surface text. But in the meaningful conversations where we want to motivate, excite, connect, and inspire, listening is so very valuable.

> Focused listening takes more time, and it requires a heavier
> emotional investment. It's not for every conversation.

When we want to go into focused listening, we first need to remember the lessons from Section 1 and be present and open-minded. When we're distracted we can't absorb the full conversation. This also means timing these conversations to create space. I love this maxim: "The right conversation at the wrong time is the wrong conversation." Both parties need to be in a place where speaking and listening will be supported. While the conversation doesn't have to be long, it also can't be rushed. I've yet to meet anyone inspired by a fifteen-second chat in the hallway while hurrying off to another meeting. Listening—and inspiring—takes focused time. But if you know what you're listening for, that time is well spent.

I've outlined four listening shifts that aid important conversations. Of course you can use them for any conversation—any time or anywhere. One listening shift may resonate more than another, or be more appropriate to a particular situation. There's no right or wrong; these are meant to be guidelines. See what works for you.

LISTENING SHIFT #1:
LISTENING FOR FACTS → LISTENING
FOR THE WHOLE PERSON

Often, when we listen we're trying to determine the facts. We go into a conversation like a police interrogation, asking for the specifics of the events so we can put it all together for ourselves. If you're like me, you may even notice that you can't hear the full situation until you have the facts out on the table. For those of us who like to think systematically and logically, the facts help us orient to the larger situation. We use the facts as a frame.

Here's where this approach limits listening: When we overfocus on the facts, we push the person talking into the background. We can easily miss the larger picture about how that person relates to the situation, what he is hoping to accomplish, or how he feels about it. Further, we know that facts are rarely pure facts. We remember them through our own filters and biases. How the speaker feels about the details is often more instructive than the details themselves.

When we home in on the facts, we push the person talking into the background.

We're better listeners if instead of zeroing in on the facts we widen our focus to take in the whole person in front of us. We discuss the facts, but we also listen for how that person explains the situation, what his body language is telling us about his emotional state. When you find yourself trying to uncover the facts, mentally stop yourself. Instead, pay attention to the person talking. Gather as much other data outside of and around the facts as you can to provide a fuller picture. Again, it's not that the facts don't matter, it's that when we focus on them exclusively, we miss important, and actionable, information.

Example: Mentoring conversation

A young professional in your office comes to you for some mentoring and guidance. He's thinking of looking for a new position inside the company. Instead of asking about whom he's spoken with, what positions he's applied for, and when he wants to move, take a step back.

Ask what's behind this desire to move. Listen to how he talks about what makes him excited, and what zaps his energy. Find out what he wants for himself longer term. The facts will likely fall naturally into the conversation, and as they do, you'll be better able to provide guidance when you can put them into the context of the whole person in front of you.

LISTENING SHIFT #2:
LISTENING FOR TEXT → LISTENING
FOR TEXT AND SUBTEXT

As we outlined earlier in the chapter, there's a whole lot of subtext going on in most conversations. Sometimes we have an idea what it might be, but we're not sure, so we don't mention it. Other times, it goes right by us. Either we choose not to bring it into the conversation because we're uncomfortable, or we fear the response, or we're distracted and oblivious.

Conversations where we aren't brave enough to be real and to say what needs to be said are never inspirational. They're superficial; they leave both parties lacking. They don't change behaviors, fix situations, or inspire people. No one feels listened to on an engaging level. They are the conversations after which we say, "Why didn't I bring that up?" or worse, "That was a waste of time."

Conversations where we aren't brave enough to be real and to say what needs to be said are never inspirational.

Learning to listen for subtext in addition to text requires a commitment to being in the moment, and to noticing both the said and the unsaid. It's paying attention to the clues the other person drops, picking them up, and probing further. It's asking questions back to gain understanding if we don't have it. It's also noting the emotional state of the other person, and bringing it into the conversation. Subtext includes the history and culture that exists around the conversation. Good listeners train their ears to hear that as well as what's spoken.

When this listening shift happens, real issues that need to be addressed get addressed. Situations are confronted, not glossed over. People listen for the meaning and get to the heart of the issue. They feel seen and heard.

Example: Feedback conversation

Let's go back to Brad and Sarah from the prior text/subtext exchange. We read what happened when both parties listened for the text: Each took the other's words at face value and moved on. (And, we can guess that nothing was going to change.) If Sarah were to listen for the subtext, she would have started the conversation more candidly, by letting Brad know that this was a serious issue. She could have listened for his reactions and pointed out that he seemed frustrated by the feedback. She might have asked him what he would be willing to do to change, and fully taken in his responses to gauge his seriousness. And—if he didn't seem to absorb the feedback—she might have asked him directly if he was committed to working with her.

For his part, Brad could have stated his confusion about what he is actually being evaluated on—his results or his relationships. He could have engaged Sarah on the impact of this feedback to his career, and determined how relevant it actually was.

LISTENING SHIFT #3:
LISTENING FOR WHAT YOU NEED →
LISTENING FOR WHAT THE OTHER PERSON
NEEDS TO SAY

Similar to listening for facts, we can default to listening for what we need from a conversation and miss what the other person needs to say. We are only partially listening to the other person, while working through a checklist in our minds. As we've seen, our internal thoughts are often louder and more prioritized than our external conversation.

When we listen this way, our agenda is the only one that matters. We're filtering out any information that doesn't conform to what we believe we need to hear. That means we're missing the other person's agenda. What's important to us supersedes what's important to the speaker. Depending on the conversation, this can negate the whole reason we're communicating with this person in the first place.

When we listen for what we need, our agenda is the one that matters.

By shifting our listening to what the other person needs to say, we're opening our own minds to the meaning of the conversation. We're sharing the agenda; we're taking in the details we deem worthy, and we're also noticing the value another places on those details. Letting the other person speak first and set the conversation's tone may help this. We may need to keep our input to a minimum, or hold it back until the end. Always, it requires us not to cut the other person off, and to encourage full expression.

Example: Buy-in conversation

A colleague comes into your office to seek your buy-in on a project she's spearheading. You've seen this project tried (and fail) before so you want to make sure the situation is different this time. You know exactly what you want to see, so your first instinct is to ask her a series of questions and listen for the responses you want to hear. You'll direct the dialogue.

By shifting your listening, however, you can withhold judgment and provide an open platform for her to express her ideas and tell you why she'd like you to support her. Rather than proactively asking whether she has covered all the bases, you say "Walk me through your thinking." You soon learn that your colleague not only covered her bases, but has conceptualized her project entirely differently than the failed approach you've seen before. You give her your support.

LISTENING SHIFT #4:
LISTENING TO JUDGE → LISTENING
OUT OF CURIOSITY

None of us wants to believe that we're judgmental. Yet, we are. After all, it's an adaptive behavior that lets us analyze efficiently. Being able to assess our environments, weigh evidence against past experience, and draw swift conclusions allows us to survive and thrive. It aids our functioning in a busy work environment, and may even be why we're good at what we do. When it comes to listening, however, that same capacity to make snap judgments can hinder our ability to understand—and show understanding of—another person.

This shift requires us to tamp down the analytical, critical part of ourselves in order to stay with the conversation, and show empathy to the other person. We need this shift when we want to learn, rather than just confirm what we already think. It means owning up to the fact that we do try to judge, and in this case, that's not our objective.

We need to shift to curiosity when we want to learn, rather than just confirm what we already think.

When we listen out of curiosity, we come in with an open mind. We focus attention on what the other person is conveying—the words she chooses, the energy she projects, and the emotions she portrays. We ask questions out of curiosity about what the other person shows us and expresses, rather than simply about what we want to know. We're not trying to guess or get it right, but to let our curiosity lead the way. A curiosity-driven conversation meanders because we're learning as we go.

Example: Missed deadline conversation

You have an employee who, in the last few months, has begun to miss deadlines. He's never had this problem before, and you've tried to be patient. But he's also getting to work late and leaving early. You're fairly certain he's checked out and interviewing for another job. You want to verify your hunch so you can prepare.

You're tempted to go into the conversation with judgmental listening, hunting for any signs that your employee isn't invested at work. However, to shift your listening into curiosity, you wipe your assumptions before the discussion. Now you aren't guided by what has happened before with other people. Instead, you go into the conversation genuinely curious to learn what's happening with *this* person. You would notice his state of being, what he brings up, and how he approaches the topic. Curious, you'd ask questions such as, "I notice that your engagement seems different—what's behind that?" or "What should I know about your current work?" or even the simple, "What would you like for me to know?"

Your only objective is to get and *stay* curious. You can make your judgments and deductions later, but in that moment, you want to learn as much as you can. And you *will* learn: When people aren't feeling judged, they are far more self-revealing.

THERE'S NO RIGHT WAY TO LISTEN . . .
BUT THERE ARE WRONG WAYS

If you went into this chapter thinking you were already a good listener, I hope this reinforced it. If you were like me, on the other hand, you may have found that listening deeply has more moving parts than you anticipated. The good news is that what we concentrate on gets stronger. If we try to listen better, the trying alone will help us.

What we concentrate on gets stronger. If we try to listen better, the trying alone will help us.

I gave you quite a few aspects of listening to consider: managing internal conversations, text versus subtext, and the reasons we don't listen well. Most of these suggestions boil down to quieting our minds and using the power of our full attention. The shifts may be helpful in certain situations to put new approaches into practice for you. Just naming what you want to do can be beneficial, for instance, "I'm going to go into this conversation with John listening for text and subtext." When we shift our thinking, we shift our listening.

In the end, there's no one right way to listen, but there are wrong ways. If we don't provide a space to listen and to take in the important information, then we may be hearing, but we're not listening. Even if we don't recognize when we're listening poorly, it's a near certainty that the other party does. When one party doesn't listen, the other party stops trying to engage.

If we're in the conversation to inspire someone, we can never underestimate the power of focused listening. I'd be willing to bet that anyone who ever inspired you also listened to you. Sometimes, that's all it takes.

TAKEAWAYS

FROM CHAPTER 6

⊙ Deep, focused listening is a key inspirational skill, but it's harder than it looks. Most people focus on hearing rather than on understanding. It takes effort, but you can become a better listener by understanding the listening environment.

⊙ Any conversation is actually multiple conversations—the ones we're stating out loud and the ones we're having with ourselves. We pay most attention to what's in our heads, especially when that's an entirely different conversation than what we're uttering. This is exacerbated by the fact that people talk far more slowly than they think.

⊙ Most conversations have both a text (what is said) and a subtext (the context that's not expressed). If we want a conversation to be inspiring and real, we need to bring the subtext into the text.

⊙ We spend far more time listening than speaking. Listening has been shown to be a prominent part of how we evaluate one another's communication effectiveness. Yet, we are rarely trained on listening skills.

⊙ To be a deeper listener, shift your listening from how you're listening to what you're listening for. These shifts include listening for the whole person rather than the facts, listening for text and subtext rather than just for text, listening for what the other person needs to say and not what you need to hear, and listening out of curiosity and not to judge.

PASSIONATE

BRINGING
HEART AND
ENERGY

CHAPTER 7

YOUR ENERGY IS CONTAGIOUS

1942 was a miserable year.

The world was enmeshed in war with unfathomable human atrocities. The Axis powers were pushing forward. Fear and hopelessness spread. Spirit and resolve, so critically needed, were in short supply. It was on the shoulders of Allied leaders to invoke a sense of fight—literally and energetically—into the populace.[1]

When the 65-year-old Winston Churchill walked into 10 Downing Street as the new prime minister he was called an old man. That impression was short lived. He became known for his tireless energy and rousing calls to action. As he said in his 1940 address to the House of Commons, with Britain's position precarious: "I have nothing to offer but blood, toil, tears and sweat."

Across the ocean, Franklin Delano Roosevelt was in his third term in office, having already spent nine grueling years ushering America through the Great Depression, fighting for his sweeping New Deal packages and establishing Social Security. Still, FDR valiantly shepherded the nation through the war, his words buttressing the spirits of a nation. His inaugural address became increasingly prescient: "the only thing we have to fear is fear itself."

Churchill and FDR are embedded in our history as two of the greatest leaders of all time. They fortified entire nations with hope and resolve. They are also known for demonstrating indefatigable energy and passionate drive. This isn't a coincidence.

Most renowned world leaders have been heralded for their energy, whether it takes the form of bombast or grinding tenacity. Consider Nelson Mandela, John F. Kennedy, British Prime Minister Margaret Thatcher, or Indian Prime Minister Indira Gandhi, to name a few. The leaders who have moved mountains have put their energy behind the push, and that energy has affected the course of history.

World leaders provide a salient example because their influence is vast, but we don't have to look that high to get the point. We know the power that energy has for all leaders. We see energy as a necessity for any person trying to inspire others, rally for a cause, or drive action. In fact, we admire it in pretty much anyone—from our friend next door who appears to have more hours in the day to the UPS guy who delivers our packages with an extra-gregarious hello. Energy signals passion.

This section of the book explores passion as an inspirational quality. It's not hard to understand: People who are passionate enthusiasts for what they do create passion in others. Passion is optimistic, exciting, bold, and captivating. Passion has a fiery drive to it, propelling forward momentum. Passionate people have an energetic field around them which others want to be caught up in. People with passion show conviction. We know where they stand. They get things done.

One of the reasons we value passion so highly is because we know how we feel when we have it. You may have had the experience where you're new to a job or selected for a coveted project, and you're in the zone: work humming, energy flowing, and creativity rolling. You feel like you can accomplish anything, like nothing will get in your way. This happens as well in our personal lives around things we truly care about, such as helping a community initiative or coaching our kid's team. We care and we show it. We're all in.

Most of us have also experienced the flip side: loss of passion. Our job has become stale or boring and we can barely concentrate enough to get through our daily work. We're over the volunteer work we once enjoyed. Even basic tasks feel like pushing a boulder up a mountain, with the wind in our faces to boot. All work is hard work. Our energy feels depleted. We say things such as, "I don't have the energy for this."

In coaching, passion is a familiar topic, coming up frequently in sessions and workshops. Here's what I've learned: Passion feels like meaning. People desperately want to find and maintain passion in their work and in their lives. Just as important, we want to work for passionate leaders. Passion is the precursor to personal investment.

Passion feels like meaning.

Inspiring people share their passion with us. Inspire Path conversations can't happen without the right level of passion—it makes them "zingy" as one of my friends says. It infuses energy into them, creating that lift we feel after an inspiring exchange.

Having heard passion discussed in so many contexts, I've broken down the factors behind our experience of passion in others.

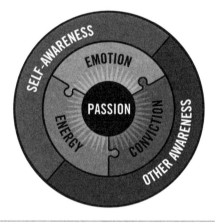

Figure 7.1: Factors in Demonstrating Passion

In the next three chapters, I'll cover in detail these elements of passion: energy, emotion, and conviction. We'll also touch upon the *right* kind of passion—just enough to energize people, but not push them away. This requires awareness of self and others, and keeping the elements of passion in check.

We'll start with energy because it's the most visible form of passion, and you might argue the one that we react to the most viscerally. It's almost as if we catch the energy of others like we would a cold—too many Debbie Downers sinks the mood. If you've ever felt that to be the case, then you're right: Energy *is* contagious. The question then becomes: What are you spreading?

Energy is the most visible form of passion.

IF THE MOOD IS SPREADING, SHOULD YOU COVER YOUR MOUTH?

Social scientists and psychologists proved long ago that *mood contagion* is a real human condition. It's been shown to spread through tone of voice, words, and nonverbal communication such as posture. In one 2000 study, participants listened to an actor read an emotionally impartial speech using either happy, sad, or neutral voice inflections. After the speech, participants were found to have moods that were congruent with the emotions expressed by the speaker. And when participants rated their attitudes toward the speaker, they said they liked the sad speaker the least.[2]

Mood contagion has been confirmed though significant research, and has been shown to spread through nonverbals, voice, words, and posture.

Studies have also shown that groups are affected by mood contagion. One study by Sigal G. Barsade at the University of Pennsylvania's Wharton School put participants into workgroups, and had actors embedded in the groups displaying high or low levels of pleasantness. The actors' positive and negative moods infected both the groups and individual group members. Further, "positive emotional contagion group members experienced improved cooperation, decreased conflict, and increased perceived task performance."[3]

As Barsade explained to me in an interview, "Emotional contagion is primarily nonverbal, but verbal also has an effect. What's insidious about emotional contagion is that people don't realize it's happening. They don't attribute their mood or behaviors as the result of someone else's mood. They own it as their own and it's almost automatic. A form of inoculation is knowing that mood contagion exists. You may still catch it but you can diminish it."[4]

Study after study overwhelmingly shows that our mood affects others. Positive or negative, people can catch it. And when the person with the strongest mood is in a position of power, the contagion is flat-out viral. If your boss comes into the office with an angry look on his face, yells at his assistant, and slams the door, the mood is going down fast.

"To the degree to which someone has power, formally or informally, and you pay more attention to them, you are more likely to catch their emotion," Barsade said. "That's why it's so important for leaders to consider what kind of emotions they're injecting into the environment. If they come in worried and stressed, even if it's not about their employees, what those employees take away is the catching of the worry and stress. Leaders have to be thoughtful about the emotions they bring in as they're constantly observed."[5]

So, our passion and energy creates passion and energy in others. It propels an emotional cycle. Researchers have found that leaders who are positive and pleasant are more likely to engage in transformational behaviors such as inspirational motivation, intellectual stimulation, and individualized consideration. Their actions lead to greater optimism, trust, and creativity.[6] This in turn creates better workplaces with passionate workers, who pass it on to their own teams. Authentically happy leaders, research would argue, are better leaders.

Passion and energy create passion and energy in others, and their opposites create the opposite.

Energy fuels people to overcome significant obstacles, which is why it's a salient issue in presidential campaigns. In companies, often the person who cares the most can push for the best results. In many organizations there's a story of one committed worker—often not even a senior leader—who pushed to change a company for the better. One of my clients, now a partner in a consulting firm, pressed his company to launch an entirely new service line even though it wasn't germane to the company's core business. His passionate belief helped him to get agreement to research the proof-of-concept, and then to secure a short-term trial. Now he's the partner in charge of an entire division, generating a sizable portion of the firm's revenue. His belief in the idea swayed others to give him a chance. If he'd been lackluster about the idea, it would have gone in the "too hard" pile.

If any mood is contagious, positive energy can be downright infectious. People borrow it from others, internalize it, and make it their own. When we're inspiring another person with our energy, that's what we're doing—lending our own passion so they can lift themselves up. Consider the phrases we use to describe inspirational communication: She "lifted my spirits," he "gave me a boost," she "pumped me up," or my personal favorite, he "gave me a kick in the pants."

When we exude positive energy, people borrow from it, internalize it, and make it their own.

The amount of energy we convey, whether in a one-on-one conversation or in front of a crowded auditorium, sets the benchmark for what other people will be able to feel. We are leading the way in showing how meaningful and important what we're communicating should be for the other person. In this way, if we don't feel it in *our*selves we can't possibly expect others to feel it in *them*selves. As one of my clients expressed after a less than enthusiastic discussion about his succession track at the company: "If they aren't excited for my future here, how can I be?"

The energy we convey sets the benchmark for what other people will be able to feel.

CONVEYING ENERGY CAN BE TRICKY

It would seem that this whole process is straightforward: We show energy, which lifts others. And yet it's tricky. We've all seen what happens when someone else's energy, even intentional and well meant, is not well received. There's an out-of-synch feeling between the energy someone's putting out and those on the receiving end. It can be off-putting and have a strong countereffect.

You may remember this happening with 2004 presidential candidate Howard Dean. Dean had been a frontrunner, but in his concession speech after losing the Iowa Caucus, he raised his voice to be heard above the noisy crowd. With his face red and sweating, he then let loose a loud scream, dubbed the "Dean Scream," which made him appear unhinged. News outlets—and then comedians—replayed the footage. It was the first time most voters had seen Howard Dean. His campaign never recovered.

I'm sure Howard Dean believed he was rousing his fans in the room to fight another day. Observers who were there recalled a raucous room with Dean supporters pumping the candidate up. But what appeared to viewers outside the room was altogether something else.[7] The energy differential was too great. Sitting on their living room sofas, having had little exposure to Dean, viewers were put off by his over-the-top enthusiasm. And unfortunately for Dean, in the age of viral information, he couldn't get past it. (Not electorally anyway, but he did reprise his scream as a show of good humor at the 2016 Democratic National Convention.)

We see this same energy gap in less conspicuous settings. A few years ago, I coached several executives in a company to get their workforce aligned behind the corporate vision. There was a new, highly passionate and positive CEO on board. When I met with him, I was hugely impressed. Full of ideas, bursting with possibilities, he left me feeling like I couldn't wait to get to work. His enthusiasm rubbed off on me. I bought in!

Then, I met his team of direct reports. It felt like someone had slammed the brakes, and hard. The team members recounted the company's dysfunctions going back a number of years and outlined the inherent problems that leadership had ignored. They were, to a person, burned out, frustrated, and negative. Their energy was so low it was catatonic. When they looked at their new CEO with his brimming enthusiasm, all they could see was naïveté. They were having corporate organ rejection of the CEO, seeing him as someone who didn't get it.

Energy is a good thing, except when it goes sideways. And showing the right amount of energy or passion can be harder than it appears. We want to be inspirational, but not over the top. We need to light a fire but not burn people out. We have to instill a sense of seriousness, but not be scary. And we mess these energy differentials up all the time.

Finding the right amount of energy or passion is critical to be in synch with our audience. And we mess these differentials up all the time.

Disclosing our energy isn't unlike self-disclosure in general. We get uncomfortable when people overshare personal information. It's TMI, as we say. When people undershare information, we can't trust them. Most people figure out how to strike the balance through trial and error as they move about socially. We try to understand—and then match— the disclosure style of the other person. If we have a colleague who keeps her feelings close to the vest, we're not going to vomit out our darkest insecurities over the watercooler. Typically, the more substantial the relationship, the more we reveal because we know how the other person will react. We test the relationship with small disclosures over time to see how sturdy and trustworthy it is. Similarly, we can test and gauge energy to see how it will be received. It requires us to notice the reactions of others and to observe how we convey our own energy.

Robert J. Vallerand, a social psychology professor at the University of Quebec and leading researcher in the area of passion, has developed a model of passion that may shed a light on why some passionate energy is attracting and some is off-putting.[8] Called the Dualistic Model of Passion, it identifies two distinct ways that we experience passion: harmonious and obsessive. People with harmonious passion enjoy their work, which they keep balanced with the rest of their life overall. When it's in their best interests to disengage from work and enjoy other activities, they can do it. Physically and psychologically healthy, they feel good about their work. High in self-esteem, they are creative, with high levels of concentration. These are the people who lift our own mood and energy. We like to be around them.

On the other hand, there are people who exhibit obsessive passion. They have an uncontrollable, knee-jerk urge to do a job, which leads them to feel more conflicted between their passion and the other activities in their lives. Obsessive passion leads to burnout and lower work satisfaction. Those who experience it tend to have lower self-esteem and exhibit more self-defensive behavior, such as aggression or overwhelm. These are the people who stress us out when we're around them.

It's a good exercise to question our own passion and see where it falls. Does your energy fuel you positively and helpfully, or does it cause stress and anxiety? If it's the latter, we're not only out of the inspiration zone, but we're harming ourselves and probably need to make some changes.

We've all known people whose energy is discomforting. Energy has great power. We should harness it and use it. We can learn to shape it to fit the inspirational tone and nature of our communication situation. We can use mood contagion to work in our favor. And finally, we should safeguard it. After all, it's not an inexhaustible resource. We have only so much of it, and when it goes, it's missed.

Energy has great power. We should harness it and use it.

CONCEPT IN ACTION

MAKING YOUR ENERGY WORK FOR YOU

Energy conveys many inspirational qualities that we like to see in our leaders, our colleagues, and our friends. It creates a ripple effect and builds followership. It's an important quality to exhibit. However, we only reap these benefits if we harness and adapt our energy to the situation and the people involved. Energy exuded well is catching; energy misfired is alienating. Here are some considerations to make sure we're spreading the right feeling around.

Know the heart of it

For other people to experience energetic passion from us, we first need to recognize it in ourselves. Often, we are going through the motions in our busy days, and when we stop to think about what we're trying to convey, it's only to get our points straight. We usually don't take the time to connect with the message, and to determine our emotional connection to it. When we want to inspire with our energy, this is the best place to start.

Finding your attachment to a message requires you to reflect on what you actually have energy around. It's getting your head and your *heart* in the game. Now you may be thinking, "Many times I have to pass along a corporate message, and it's not even mine! I don't actually feel anything about it." And I would respond that if you don't care, then it's likely that no one else will care either. It's only by seeing the energy that you bring that others adjust their own energy. That's why it's contagious.

Here's an example: I've coached many leaders at consulting firms over the years. As part of moving up in the ranks, consulting professionals need to learn how to sell and bring in new clients. Many people dislike this part of firm life. They got into consulting as subject matter experts in areas like finance or IT, and now they have to go out in the market and sell. They aren't salespeople, and they don't want to be salespeople. Consulting firms offer all kinds of training to help workers develop business and learn the skills to close deals as they approach senior ranks. Still, it's hard to get past the fact that many consulting professionals don't like to sell. And as we've been discussing, that shows.

In coaching consultants, I've seen one factor make the difference: when clients can communicate their emotional connection to what they're selling. When they are able to feel truly energized and passionate about the content, selling no longer feels like heavy lifting. Then, many of their insecurities and fears fall away.

I think about a consultant in technology who was fired up about her firm's solution to cybersecurity, or one in finance absolutely convinced that his firm could help stabilize the mortgage industry. When you go into the market with that kind of positive energy, others gravitate toward it. Just going to more networking events and handing out business cards isn't enough. You have to believe strongly in what you're selling. When you connect to that emotional core, you exhibit a mobilizing force.

When you connect to the emotional core of your message, you exhibit a mobilizing force.

I use this sales example, but it's the same effect when we're delivering a personal message one-on-one to inspire action, or to a group to gain buy-in. The act is the same: When we connect emotionally with the message, the energy comes naturally.

A good way to get clear and systematic about your energy is to make a situational intention around it, as we discussed in Chapter 2. Take a step back, pause, and consider: *What gives me energy about this? What do I want my audience to feel?* When you can identify what you feel most passionate about, what hits home, where you have the most conviction, or what's at the heart of the message—then you can craft your communication to show the authentic energy you have for the message and the audience. The more in touch you are with a message, the easier it will be to convey it with resonance to another.

Calibrate your energy to your environment

Once you know where your authentic passion lies, you'll need to calibrate it against the situation before you. As I outlined above, you don't want to be so far away from your audience that they reject your message. Don't be like the CEO who came off as a Pollyanna to a staff wallowing in negativity. Energy is a persuasive force. Use it as a tool of forward momentum to bring others along.

One way to think about this is to consider your energy on a scale of one to ten, and to do the same for your audience. Then, aim for an energy level that's the average of those two scores. So if I am trying to persuade an employee to take on a new project, I may be a ten (very enthusiastic) and she may be a two (pretty skeptical). In order for her to hear me, I can dial my own energy down to a six. If I go in as a full ten, guns blazing, I run the risk of shutting her down. Instead, I aspire to model energy, but in a way that brings her along.

Now for the caveats: You might not always know another person's energy level, and she might not be forthcoming. If that's the case, take the easiest approach and ask! See what you can learn. If it's a group, the individual members may differ. You can query the group as well. This isn't an exact science. You have to use your intuition. Look for clues as you go. Receptive body language, heads nodding, and attention are good indicators of engagement. Posture is also a clue. Are people leaning toward you or pushing themselves away? When someone's energy is too much for us, we often subconsciously get distance however we can.

Inspiring conversations create energy, but only if the other party lets them in. By calibrating your energy to the situation, while still infusing it, you create the connection that allows that spark to catch.

By calibrating your energy to the situation, while still infusing it, you create the connection that allows that spark to catch.

Put your energy on display

For some people, showing energy is straightforward. Their energy pours right from them. You know what they care about because it's written all over their faces. It animates their body language. In others, it's not so easy to discern. Either purposefully or unintentionally, they play their cards closer to the vest. They may not show their emotions readily, or express themselves very well. Sure, this type of reserve can work well in poker, but it interferes big time with an effort to infuse energy into a situation.

In business settings where we want to inspire, for the most part leaders need to emote more. We're trained to show such stoicism and equanimity that others often miss what is meaningful to us. When we're uncomfortable or nervous, we can become practically robotic. I've seen clients deliver spectacular news in a tone that connotes absolute neutrality, leaving everyone to wonder if it was good news at all. When I worked in PR, I would train leaders to speak with the media. You'd be surprised—or since you've seen them, maybe not—how non-emotive leaders can be on camera. It's as if someone zapped their personalities. You can't tell if what they're saying is good news, bad news, or means anything to them at all. This gets worse with earnings news in an effort to appear staid, leaving one wondering whether the CEO is happy about the quarter. (If you can't get to sleep, tune into corporate earnings webcasts.)

Leaders need to emote more, not less. We're trained to show such stoicism and equanimity that others often miss what is meaningful to us.

For many reading this, if you take the time to understand what you care about, then you'll be able to touch upon and show your energy readily. For others, it may be helpful to consider how we convey passion in a way that others can read. People project energy by:

- Speaking at an energetic rate of speech, rather than slowly and methodically
- Using voice inflection and vocal variety instead of a monotone
- Smiling authentically with their mouth and eyes

- Animating their gestures, often using large ones to underscore points
- Selecting energetic words that punctuate their enthusiasm, such as confident, excited, delighted, surprised, optimistic, positive, ready, pumped, energized, thrilled

If you're wondering where you fall in displaying energy, ask someone for feedback or view yourself on videotape. With a critical eye, determine how much energy you bring to a situation that you care about. If you determine that your affect is flatter than you mean it to be, take one of the bulleted points above and try to do more of it. Don't know where to start? I'd suggest making sure to smile more when communicating the positive. It's an instant way to show that what you're saying lights a fire in you—and can in others. (More on applying all of these bullet points in the next two chapters.)

Create attractor energy

In work situations, we do many hard things: We ask people to take risks, change behaviors, follow a vision, work harder, and hit goals. Without a driving energy, any of these become exponentially more challenging. As a leader, you are the one who models how much energy others should have for the task. They will care only as much as they see that you care. Your energy is a powerful tool of inspiration. Others see it and take it on, even beyond their awareness. Learn to harness your energy: Notice it, cultivate it, adapt it, and share it.

Energy creates more energy. It has an attractor quality—bringing people to us and to each other.

TAKEAWAYS

FROM CHAPTER 7

⊙ Energy is a primary way that we convey passion. We want to see passionate energy in our leaders and we view it as a requirement for being able to get things done. Further, our energy shows others how much they should care, and in effect, sets the benchmark.

⊙ Significant research has proven that mood is contagious— whether shared intentionally or accidentally. Positive mood contagion is linked to better task performance, decreased conflict, greater collaboration, and transformational leadership.

⊙ Someone else's energy can range from exhilarating to off-putting. We need to calibrate our energy to the situation and the audience. Aim for the average of where you are and where your audience is. In other words, meet them in the middle.

⊙ All passion isn't equal. There is harmonious passion, which lifts people up. We choose the activities that bring it, and can easily walk away from them. On the flip side, there's obsessive passion, the kind of passion that brings stress.

⊙ Energy is a tool we can harness and cultivate to great effect. To do so, first know what gives you energy about your message, synch that up with your audience, and display your passion verbally and nonverbally.

CHAPTER 8

MOVING HEARTS BEFORE MINDS

"You're very emotional."

That doesn't sound like a compliment, does it?

Emotion is generally the opposite of what we're striving to show. In the workplace, and to a larger extent in life, we don't feel free to express ourselves emotionally. There are plenty of cultural signals, organizational cues, and straightforward warnings that tell us we should guard against emotionality. Instead, as we discussed around authenticity, we typically strive for a well-practiced stoicism at work, keeping our emotions in constant check. Any lapse in our composure feels like a character flaw.

And yet, as we consider passion, it is inherently emotional. In fact, passion *is* an emotional state. The Oxford English Dictionary defines passion as "a strong and barely controllable emotion." Enthusiasm without emotion comes across as flat or disingenuous—not very passionate at all. It's the emotion that lets us know what's real. If we want to have an Inspire Path conversation where our passion for the person or situation comes through, then it requires us to rethink how we show our emotions.

Similar to energy, in an effort to engage with emotion, we have to calibrate. I'm not talking about sobbing openly or rampaging through the office. Clearly, these behaviors are off-putting. But I am talking about being willing to show and use emotion authentically *and* strategically to project a passionate commitment. Going back to the passion breakdown in Figure 7.1, this requires awareness of one's self and of others to determine the right balance.

Whether you're comfortable showing emotion or not, the reality is that we are all intensely emotional beings. It's how we show our humanity, and how we communicate empathy. Emotion has an effect on others that words alone can never have.

We are all intensely emotional beings. It's how we show our humanity, and how we communicate empathy.

I'm reminded of this when delivering keynote speeches. Like everyone else, I've ingrained the practice of keeping my emotions contained and exhibiting calm. My early training was around cultivating a polished presence. Yet I have to go against that training to connect with my audience. I know the more I share of myself and allow myself to be real the more the audience can identify with me. One of the ways I push myself is to use stories that have deep meaning to me. In the telling, my true emotions come through—sometimes they even get ahead of me. My voice will shake, or my face will flush. It's not planned; I can never tell when it will happen. A few weeks ago I read a line from a poem about courage that I'd read at my grandmother's funeral. It didn't affect me at all when I rehearsed it, but when I was on the stage it hit me in the chest. My voice thinned, and I could feel my emotions rising. My first instinct was to be embarrassed for losing composure. But then people came up to me after the talk and thanked me for what I shared. They told their own stories, which were similar to mine. They connected with me in a meaningful way. The real, emotional, human stuff is what has the most impact—every single time.

When we share our emotions, we allow others to share theirs. The emotions are already there, inside them, unexpressed. It's the observing of emotions in someone else that brings them to the surface. In Chapter 4, we discussed authenticity at length. It makes sense that revealing our emotions is part of how we show others who we are. It's reflected in PepsiCo CEO Indra Nooyi's discussion of being wholehearted at work. When we can reveal an emotional side to ourselves and to our message, we bring head and heart into it. It resonates in a more meaningful and personal way.

When we share our emotions, we allow others to share theirs.

I understand that I'm going against some readers' longheld beliefs by suggesting that we show more emotion, especially in business. Stay with me. Remember, we're in a conversation about passion, inspiration, and connection. We're talking about communicating in a way that gets people to make big changes, tackle tough challenges, or fully invest themselves. These kinds of actions are dripping with emotion, either holding you back or propelling you forward—whether or not you even know it. Emotions are guiding our choices and pervading our thoughts all the time. This chapter will discuss what underlies this dynamic, and how we can put emotion in service to our boldest goals.

Big actions are dripping with emotion, either holding you back or propelling you forward—whether or not you even know it.

YOU'RE EMOTIONAL EVEN WHEN
YOU'RE TRYING NOT TO BE

In Chapter 3 we explored the myriad of cognitive biases that invade our thinking and preclude us from making logical decisions. Recall how Daniel Kahneman's concept of System 1 and System 2 work. Our minds are trained to make snap judgments based on cognitive biases and historical experiences (System 1) which only get confronted when something requires further analysis from System 2. Further, we make decisions and operate in the world through a veil of irrational biases. Duke University professor and behavioral economist Dan Ariely, in *Predictably Irrational*, argues that, by and large, we don't even know what's impacting our decisions.[1] In Chapter 3 I outlined several biases, such as recency bias and confirmation bias, but these are only the tip of the iceberg.

Social psychologist and New York University professor Jonathan Haidt, who studies morality and emotion in people and systems, coined a popular phrase in behavioral economics and neuroscience circles: "The emotional tail wags the rational dog."[2] Based on his research, Haidt argues that we make decisions emotionally and then justify them with logic. For example: "I feel nervous to present my idea so it must not be ready." He calls this phenomenon *social intuitionism* and argues that it has far-reaching consequences in how we arrive at decisions and opinions. First we intuit, and then we contrive moral judgments that support that intuition. Haidt believes that the intuition part isn't actually reasoning, but a knee-jerk emotional response that we often can't explain.

"The emotional tail wags the rational dog."

Some convictions are so deeply held that we can't logically explain them at all. Haidt calls this *moral dumbfounding*. In his research, Haidt set up examples of situations where participants couldn't articulate the reasoning behind a strongly held conviction (like why it's repugnant to give a starving person a dead pet to eat). Then he asked the participants to explain their visceral disgust. He provided a rational answer for each reaction, for instance, "We eat farm animals that are pets; people in other countries believe it's normal to eat the same animal." Finally, this leads the participants to say, "I can't explain it, but it's just wrong!"[3] This isn't to say that we should get people to change their minds about repugnant situations, just that some decisions are made from pure emotion, with logic left out of the picture.

It's not only in offensive situations where you can see this kind of emotional conclusion without a rational argument. Just look at elections. It's widely known in political circles that people decide whom they're going to vote for emotionally, and then justify it through factual reasoning. This is why likeability is of huge concern to candidates, and a primary area of polling. This kind of moral dumbfounding makes it nearly impossible to change someone's mind about their preferred candidate—unless new, overwhelming, contrasting evidence causes them to reflect on their decision. That's why you can't get your Uncle Dan to change his vote, even with a vociferous and well-documented case for why he's wrong. Not to mention, why posting political comments on social media is a useless exercise.

HAVE I GOT A STORY FOR YOU

Emotion is a key part of how we process information, and while it can get in the way of logic, it also makes us care. Without emotion there is no empathy. Our emotional responses call upon the deepest parts of our humanity. Look at how charities encourage you to give money. They put images of starving families on the screen, or interview children visibly stricken with cancer. In 2015, St. Jude's Children's Research Hospital ran a holiday campaign asking for donations to "give

thanks for the healthy children in your life and those who are not"—
bringing to mind the loved ones you hold dearest. It worked on me: I
sent money.

Emotion gets in the way of logic, but it also makes us care.

Pulitzer Prize–winning *New York Times* columnist Nicholas Kristof
travels to the darkest places around the globe to document horrendous
crimes and suffering. His aim is to make people care. For example, he
tries to shake readers out of complacency about millions of displaced
war refugees by showing the impact on individual families who are not
so different than his comfortable readers.

In the HBO documentary *Reporter,* Kristof describes how he's
driven to find relatable, memorable stories in his travels.[4] He's found
that people aren't affected by statistics, and in fact, overwhelming
numbers have a numbing effect. "How can I make a dent in helping
795 million hungry people in the world?" we ask. Instead, he finds the
most gripping stories to share, which incite discussion and mobilize
people to help. You may recall the reaction in 2015 when the image of
the drowned toddler off the coast of Turkey generated an international
outcry to deal with the Syrian refugee crisis. It took that emotional,
horrific image to instigate global awareness.

Stories have a unique way of hitting an emotional and resonant
chord. We discussed in Chapter 4 how stories convey authenticity. Part
of the reason is that a good story evokes emotion. And in fact, stories
do much more than that.

Neuroeconomist Paul J. Zak studies how our brain processes support virtuous behaviors such as trustworthiness, generosity, and sacrifice. As part of that work, he's researched the human reaction to
stories.[5] Zak finds that stories attain their power in several significant ways. First, they command our brain's attention and focus,
which are very limited resources. Second, they invoke emotion,

which causes empathy. This makes us care about the other person, uses more of our brain function, and enhances retention. Third, we've evolved to pay attention to stories for our own learning. Similar to a "car accident effect" we zero in to see if there's something we need to learn to protect ourselves. Finally, when we listen to stories, our brain releases oxytocin, also dubbed the "love hormone." Oxytocin enhances our sense of trust and empathy; it makes us feel that we can safely approach others.

Stories change how we listen, and how well we listen. They also enhance trust.

Zak argues that oxytocin is central to our reaction to stories. In his research, he's studied the effects when people are given even a synthetic version of oxytocin via nasal spray. In one such study, participants were given the synthetic oxytocin while viewing various public service ads from charities. Those given the oxytocin donated to 57 percent more of the featured charities and gave 56 percent more money than the participants given the placebo.[6]

Luckily, we don't need to put oxytocin up people's noses to get them to care. All we have to do is tell a great story and let nature take its course.

ARISTOTLE SAID IT FIRST

Many years ago, in my graduate program in communications at Purdue University, I was unhappy to learn that everyone had to take the rhetoric course. I was there to study political behavior and persuasion, not fourth-century debate style, which seemed antiquated and irrelevant. Nonetheless, I ended up learning foundational elements of rhetorical persuasion that have stayed with me. One is known as Aristotle's modes of persuasion, often called the rhetorical triangle, seen in Figure 8.1.

Aristotle argued in his treatise that we are most persuasive when we combine all of these elements. Yes, logic and reason have a role. Presenting oneself as credible and authoritative is key too. And, as you can see, emotion has an equally important place in persuasion. It's not an either/or scenario. We're most likely to change minds when we can speak to both the head and the heart.

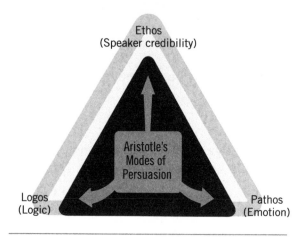

Figure 8.1: Aristotle's Modes of Persuasion

So let's bring this back to passion or, to our larger mission, inspiration. We, too, have more than one tool at our disposal. When we can put our own heart behind our message, we bring emotion out in others. It has a contagion effect. Even when our Inspire Path conversation is quieter, with more listening than orating, emotion still plays a role. By sharing our own feelings, we connect on an emotional level.

Now, let's talk about how to turn this idea into action.

CONCEPT IN ACTION

GETTING TO THE HEART OF THE MATTER

Before we jump into tactics, it's worth noting that some may feel ambivalent or disdainful about purposefully tapping into their own and other people's emotions. It's understandable. After all, we've made considerable efforts to show up as unflappable and logical. Culturally, making an emotional case can feel sleazy and wrong, as if we're trying to trick someone. And certainly world history is littered with despots who played dirty through the use of emotions.

So let's frame the situation up front: When we bring emotion into our Inspire Path conversations, we're not faking or manipulating. We're authentically communicating the emotions that we already possess. We're bringing to the surface the emotions of others—which are guiding their decisions and thoughts already. In short, we're communicating in a wholehearted way.

> When we bring emotion into our Inspire Path conversations, we're not manipulating. We're authentically communicating the emotions that we already possess.

Consider three ways to infuse your communications with more emotion: emotional appeals, emotional language, and storytelling.

INCLUDE AN EMOTIONAL APPEAL

Going back to Aristotle's rhetorical triangle, one way to ensure you're touching upon the emotional side of communications is to ensure that you have an emotional appeal. Our go-to appeal is logic. We think through our main points, and form a coherent argument for what we want to say. Especially when communicating with those who don't know us well, we also demonstrate our credibility by highlighting our expertise and background. This is what introductions are all about. Yet, we leave out the emotional appeal—and this is the part that brings the passion to our words.

There is no one right way to make an emotional appeal, but Robert Cialdini's model in Chapter 3 provides a handy and useful one.[7] Cialdini outlined six principles of influence, each of which can convert into straightforward, inspiring emotional appeals. Again, these could be in the domain of shifty advertisers trying to get our money, as Cialdini cautions. But there's another side to emotional appeals as well. They can come from a place of positivity and inspiration.

PRINCIPLE OF PERSUASION	EMOTIONAL APPEAL COULD BE . . .
Appeal to Authority	"We have the history and expertise to tackle this challenge."
	"I'm asking you as your leader to stand with me on this."
Appeal to Scarcity	"Time is of the essence. This is our chance to show the market what we can do."
	"We've got one year to turn this company around. Let's rise to the challenge."
Appeal to Reciprocity	"I've always had your back. Will you support me in a promotion to this role?"
	"I was glad to make the introduction to my colleague a few years back when you were looking for a new position. Would you mind connecting me to John in your network?"
Appeal to Consistency and Commitment	"You've said before that you admire our culture. I'm asking you to spread the word to help us recruit."
	"You've mentioned how much you appreciate the trust between us. I'd like your honesty now about this issue."

PRINCIPLE OF PERSUASION	EMOTIONAL APPEAL COULD BE . . .
Appeal to Liking	"We have a long shared history. I hope that we can speak as friends." "I started as an intern here, just like many of you. I understand where you're coming from."
Appeal to Social Proof	"95 percent of our employees volunteer their time in the community. Won't you join us?" "Every member of senior management has taken a pay cut, including me. We ask everyone to share in reducing costs."

The emotional appeal doesn't have to be complex and it doesn't have to dominate the discussion. Just considering the emotional component that you want to convey and putting it on the table brings relevance to the conversation. The emotional appeal can frame the conversation; it can be an impactful point or a takeaway. For example, you may want to set a tone of collegiality by reminding someone of your shared history through anecdotes. You will find, however, that most passionate speeches—and our most memorable conversations—have a strong emotional appeal to them. They touch us, and because of that, we remember them.

The emotional appeal can frame the conversation; it can be an impactful point or a takeaway. It can also be an intention that gets subtly conveyed.

SPEAK WITH EMOTION WORDS

Another way that we can convey emotion is literal: We can use emotion words. Emotion words tell the receiver what the speaker is feeling personally, or wants the other party to feel. Because emotions are always swirling under the surface anyway, emotion words can provide language to those thoughts and feelings. In Chapter 2 we discussed the dichotomy of motivating behavior coming from a place of love or fear. Emotion words can be uplifting. Or they can give voice to fear, so that it can be tackled at its core. Language is generative: It creates meaning which gets passed along, creating meaning for others.

Emotion words tell the receiver what the speaker is feeling personally, or wants the other party to feel.

Not all language is created equal. When a speaker gets up and goes through thirty slides of facts and figures our emotional reaction is dulled. When that same speaker shares her feelings behind the facts and figures, provides anecdotes that elicit excitement or concern, and uses strong emotional words to cue our own responses, then we have a fuller, multisensory experience. It's the difference between:

Let me lay out all of the facts to show you why this plan will work. (Non-emotive language)

and . . .

I have absolute confidence that we're prepared and ready. Here's why I'm excited. (Emotive language)

Usually the most convincing argument isn't an either/or but rather a both/and, as Aristotle so eloquently showed. Provide the logic, and underscore it with emotion.

Most of the non-emotive leaders I work with know they aren't engaging, but they can't figure out what to do about it. One simple fix is to help them inject their conversation with emotion words. Instead of only conveying the facts, share the emotion behind those facts. Figure 8.2 may provide some ideas for how to put more emotion words into your communication. The most common emotions that leaders try to convey and instill in others are confidence, joy, anger and urgency. At first anger may seem like a risky emotion to show, but it's an important one. Leaders may need to express frustration at a situation, show disappointment at a problem, or call out a wrong. Researchers have found that moral anger has a strong positive role in organizations.[8] Think about whistleblowers or leaders who go to the mat for their teams.

If you're trying to convey an emotion, see if any of these words help it to take shape. How many of them are already a regular part of your dialogue? If not many, use this list to help crystalize your next conversation. Sometimes, what we're missing is just the right word.

Figure 8.2: Emotion Words for Inspired Conversations

TELLING AN EMOTIONAL STORY

In this book, we've touched upon stories in a couple of different ways. In Chapter 2, we talked about how our embedded stories can hold us hostage and inhibit growth. In Chapter 4, we discussed how to illuminate authenticity by sharing leadership stories. What makes stories powerful, either positively or negatively, is that they carry emotional weight. Stories are an inspirational tool that we can cultivate to bring passion and emotion to Inspire Path conversations.

Storytelling has significant impacts: focusing our attention, providing clarity, enhancing retention, and eliciting trust. You probably already know you should incorporate stories into your repertoire. Most leaders I've met agree they should tell more stories because they've been told storytelling is a leadership attribute. Yet, when I ask leaders in an audience to raise their hands if they think they're good storytellers, few brave souls do. And when I asked why they feel unskilled at telling stories, they say they:

- Aren't sure how to tell a good story
- Lack the right skills and tend to mess up the delivery
- Don't know what a listener would find interesting
- Forget about it in the moment

The attention on storytelling in the leadership development industry is warranted, but there's an unintended consequence: it's turned something natural and intuitive into a seemingly difficult skill. If you need a two-day workshop to learn how to do it, it must be hard to master! It's enough to make good storytellers doubt themselves.

Storytelling requires no advanced skills. You have everything you need already—your voice plus your experiences.

Storytelling requires no advanced skills. You already have everything you need—your voice and your experiences. Effective stories can be long or short, fact-based or anecdotal. For stories to affect us emotionally they need to have just a few elements. I provided this model in *The Power of Presence* and have used it frequently with clients. It clicks storytelling into place for most people, and empowers them by showing how simple it actually is. (After introducing it to an audience with a few minutes to practice, nearly all hands are raised when I ask again who's a good storyteller. I kid you not. It's that easy.)

A good story has:

- **A clear moral or purpose**—there's a reason why you're telling this story to this audience at this time.
- **A personal connection**—the story involves either you or someone you feel connected to.
- **Common reference points**—the audience understands the context and situation of the story.
- **Detailed characters and imagery**—there's enough visual description that we can create a picture of what you're seeing.
- **Conflict, vulnerability, or achievement we can relate to**—there's action to the story, with challenges revealed and acted upon in a context we understand.
- **Pacing**—there's a clear beginning, ending, and segue back to the topic.

That's it! There's no magic formula beyond this. You can play around with the elements, such as providing more or less detail, but a story structure doesn't need anything else.

Stories evoke emotion by their very nature. You can think about telling stories whenever you want to lead, inspire, or motivate others, create trust, or show connection. Good times to tell stories include when you are:

- Motivating people around important initiatives, culture, or strategies
- Simplifying complexity and aiding in retention
- Building trust with people who don't know you
- Helping people change
- Getting others to personally invest in an idea
- Allowing others to know your leadership style, expectations, and values

Beyond how and when to tell a story, it may be helpful to consider the variety of stories you can tell. I created this rubric for my executive clients to encourage them to think broadly about the types of stories they currently tell, and how to stretch themselves. You may find that you tell stories, but only a certain kind. Leaders can use stories in myriad situations. Consider which ones you may use now, and can incorporate in the future.

Stories Leaders Can Tell

Challenge Stories: "We can do this."
Relating Stories: "I get you. You get me."
Metaphoric Stories: "Let's look at it a different way."
Vision Stories: "Imagine what we could do."
Potential Stories: "Think where you'll be next year."
Cautionary Tales: "Let's not make that mistake."
Humorous Stories: "Let's keep perspective."

Now that you have this material, hopefully, you can see a path to tell more stories like the leaders in my workshops. And when you do, you'll see their impact by the reaction the stories get, what they bring out in others, and how they connect your audience to you.

As a plus, you won't have to memorize stories to tell. After all, you already know them.

EMOTIONS IN SERVICE TO _____.

"You're very emotional" may still not seem like a compliment, but it is a truism. We are emotional beings, and we respond to emotions with emotions. If we're having Inspire Path conversations, emotion makes them more real, more resonant, and more passionate. Our emotions are guiding our thoughts and actions always, and by thinking about emotions strategically, we can put them in service to our most inspired goals. Instead of making emotions something we hide or tamp down, consider how they can support your message. How can emotions be strategic and in service to you? What emotion do you want to impart? By crafting our communications to be both logical and emotional, we truly can inspire with head and heart.

TAKEAWAYS

FROM CHAPTER 8

⊙ There is no passion without emotion, and any attempt to convey such comes across unconvincing or deceptive. Emotion tells others what's real to us. Yet, we've been taught that showing emotion is a sign of weakness.

⊙ Sharing our emotions allows others to share theirs in return, and encourages personal investment. Inspiring others to change or grow requires an emotional investment on both sides—the communicator and the receiver.

⊙ We're emotional beings, whether we want to be or not. Research shows that emotions drive many of our decisions which we rationalize with logic after the fact—hence the saying, "the emotional tail wags the rational dog." Some decisions are based in emotion to the extent that we can't even explain them with logic.

⊙ Stories have a strong emotional pull on us. They have been shown to increase a listener's focus and attention, invoke empathy, and release oxytocin, which creates trust.

⊙ Being strategic and authentic with emotions in our communications helps us to inspire others. Three ways to do this are by making emotional appeals, by using emotion words, and by telling engaging stories.

CHAPTER 9

SAY IT LIKE YOU MEAN IT

A common lament I hear from CEOs and senior leaders is how visible they're expected to be. The need seems unending, as if it's never enough. There's a perception chasm between how much leaders feel that they're communicating and how little their teams believe they are. I've heard CEOs who have come up through the ranks of the same organization they're currently leading express surprise and exasperation at the pressing need to be seen so often and so deeply in such a personal, human way by people who they thought already knew them. It can be overwhelming, especially for reserved personalities. But people need to see for themselves what the leader believes.

Early in my career, I did a short stint in marketing for a media company in the midst of a turnaround situation. A venerable institution, the company had been in decline for years, and a new CEO had been brought in to transform the business from the ground up. Everyone knew, from the old timers to the new folks like me, that this required exquisite vision, precise execution, and an intense amount of fortitude.

In those early days of the CEO's tenure, when he held town hall meetings on the main floor, the room was packed. These were not-to-miss events. People would stand on desks and chairs to physically see the CEO speak. They wanted to see his conviction. Did he have what it took to make the company a success?

Some employees who'd been there for decades had witnessed numerous failed attempts to resurrect the company, with leaders coming in full of promise only to exit swiftly and quietly. The employees wanted to see whether this CEO had true conviction. It wasn't enough to hear it—they needed to witness it. I can still sense the intense focus in that room. (In case you're wondering, it didn't work out and the company was eventually sold.)

At this point, I've had a behind-the-curtain seat at dozens and dozens of companies going through major changes, from risky startups to established corporations. What stays consistent is the very human need we have to see for ourselves how much conviction our leaders actually possess. We can't invest until we see it. It's not enough to read it in a well-crafted email or to have someone relay it to us. We are the final arbiters of our own buy-in.

We need to see for ourselves how much conviction our leaders have. We can't invest until we see it.

Conviction is the last component of passion. It's the closer. We engage through our energy, we deepen the connection with emotion, and we show our mettle through conviction. When we seek to inspire others, we are encouraging them to believe. When we demonstrate conviction, we show that we already believe wholeheartedly, making it safer for others to take that leap. As with passion, when we show our own conviction, we are lending it out to another. Such as in this exchange:

"Do you think I can actually get that promotion?"

"Do I think you can? I know you can. You've worked hard, you deserve it, and I have zero doubt that you are the best candidate. Go for it!"

"Maybe you're right. I have worked hard for this."

When you imagine that conversation, you could probably hear a certain tone behind the words or even visualize the nonverbal communication of the people speaking. If I asked what someone showing conviction looks like, you could likely conjure a series of images in your mind. Maybe you even saw a certain principled person that you know.

Conviction: We recognize it when we see it. One of the primary places that we look for this quality is in nonverbal communication. It's not enough to speak with conviction; we also want to see it reflected. This chapter will cover how to project conviction through our entire presence.

THE NONVERBAL
COMMUNICATION QUAGMIRE

You can't escape a class or training about communication skills without hearing the importance of nonverbal communication. Experts give all kinds of (often contradictory) advice about what kind of nonverbal communication is the best. Some recommendations are ad hoc, while others are based on the decades of formal studies. Social scientists have produced voluminous amounts of research on the relationship of nonverbals to communicating power, trustworthiness, and influence.

Perhaps the most cited nonverbal research—often without correct attribution or a full understanding—is that of UCLA psychology professor Albert Mehrabian from his studies in the 1960s.[1] You've probably seen the "55/38/7" rule that when we communicate, 55 percent is communicated through facial expressions, 38 percent through tone of voice, and only 7 percent through words. As I wrote about in *The Power of Presence*, Mehrabian has attempted to rein in decades of misinterpretation by explaining that his research was limited to a narrow situation when the communicator was speaking about his like or dislike of something.[2] Regardless, these figures get continuously invoked to make the case that nonverbals are running the impression show.

In fact, nonverbal communication, and its interpretation, is extremely complex and nuanced. What is included in nonverbal communication exactly? Where does verbal communication stop and nonverbal begin? Communicators are evaluated on a spectrum of behaviors, including words, tone, facial expressions, gestures, posture, touch, spatial distance, and appearance. One Harvard study focused on nonverbal expression and power identified seventy distinct nonverbal behaviors and skills that people evaluate.[3]

Communicators are evaluated on a spectrum of behaviors, including words, tone, facial expressions, gestures, posture, touch, spatial distance, and appearance.

When trying to improve as a communicator, it's no wonder that people get stuck on nonverbals and body language. It's a tough nut to crack! While it gets considerable attention, there are contradictory guidelines, further nuanced by human complexity. When I'm speaking about presence, audience questions about nonverbals are ubiquitous. I've had more than a few coaching clients request "checklists" of the most powerful nonverbals.

And this is what I have to tell them: There is no right way to stand, gesture, speak, touch, or even dress. It all depends.

Now I know this is probably not what you want to hear. But think about it. Have you ever seen someone deliver a presentation with all the correct body language—perfect posture, considered pauses, big gestures—and yet there was no connection? Or have you seen the reverse? Look at some of the most viewed TED Talks. While the speakers are engaging, they aren't professional orators by any means. Their nonverbal styles vary widely. What they have in common is that they're authentic and engaged.

So, how do you say it like you mean it? It comes down to alignment. You need your nonverbals to match your words, and both to match your intent. If we want to show conviction, verbal and nonverbal should support each other, not create noisy static. That's the aim. Yes, body language matters, but so does the context. And so does your personality. How you do it doesn't have to be how I do it. Culture plays a role, as does individuality. I'll never forget the woman I coached who, after moving to the New York office from Asia, had been told she should make large gestures to show power, even though this was in direct opposition to how she was raised and to her quiet nature. (You can guess that I told her to ignore the advice and find her own way.)

When we show conviction our nonverbals match our words and both match our intent.

Given my background, you may be surprised to hear that I struggle with how much emphasis to give to nonverbal communications. I see how people get fixated on the wrong things, and risk coming across with less conviction and far less authenticity. I also realize that there's a desire to get clearer and be more effective in this area. As a continual surprise to me, a piece I wrote for *Forbes* in 2012 called "Confessions of a Former Public Speaking Trainer: Don't Waste Your Money" remains the most-read article I've published. In it, I argue that we've placed an overreliance on technique at the expense of conviction. Guess I'm not the only one thinking that.

Yes, we want clarity. What's the best way to manage nonverbal communications to get our messages across? Knowledge helps us make informed choices. In this chapter, as we discuss how to show conviction, this feels like an important conversation to have. So, let's talk about how to avoid getting stuck in the nonverbal quagmire, how to know the boundaries—based on research, not hearsay—and how to chart one's own path. I'll share some concepts that I've found to be most helpful around nonverbal communications, and provide ways to put your whole self behind your message. You show conviction when you speak with clarity, alignment, and full-body presence. You can decide what that looks like for you, in any particular situation.

START BY REALIZING WHAT YOU THINK YOU KNOW IS PROBABLY WRONG

In Chapter 4, we discussed the psychological phenomenon of the *transparency illusion,* which says that we overestimate how much others understand about what we're feeling. We believe our thoughts are written all over us—when in fact, we're quite opaque.

Overconfidence comes into play when we're reading other people, too, says David DeSteno, a psychology professor at Northeastern University who studies physical signs of trustworthiness. "Researchers in the academic, business, and military communities have spent years trying to uncover a few simple methods for detecting trustworthiness but, despite their best efforts, continue to come up short. . . . And, as a recent report by the Government Accounting Office revealed, even the tactics Homeland Security and TSA agents are trained to use don't work reliably."[4]

DeSteno and other researchers in the field have found that when it comes to reading body language, we actually look at clusters. For example, it's not just the lack of eye contact, but also the shoulders hunched and the turning away of the face, that tell us someone isn't on our page. Additionally, we take context into account. If I'm sitting in front of you sweating, you may believe that I'm anxious. But if you learn that the elevator is broken and I just climbed eight flights of stairs, then your opinion swiftly changes.

When it comes to reading another's body language, we look at clusters of behaviors. Context also plays a role.

DeSteno conducted an experiment to determine what cluster of nonverbal communication behaviors signaled untrustworthiness in another person. He found four nonverbal acts—leaning away from a partner, crossing one's arms, hand touching, and face touching—were reliable indicators of untrustworthiness, but only *when occurring together.*[5] One act alone didn't count; it was the cluster that mattered. DeSteno found this effect to be so reliable that he was even able to replicate it by using humanoid robots programmed to show the same nonverbal signals. Participants who saw the robots exhibit those four behaviors reported trusting them less.

An interesting sidenote: DeSteno found that participants couldn't exactly identify what behaviors caused them to trust or not trust someone. He also reported that people actually talk themselves out of their initial impressions through rationalization and logic. "I had a bad feeling after interviewing John, but he was recommended by Sally, so I must be wrong."

There's evidence that even when we read body language correctly we rationalize ourselves out of those impressions.

Other research has shown that people are overconfident and over-reliant on facial expressions. We believe that if we can "see it in their face" then we'll know with certainty. But a study conducted at Princeton suggested otherwise. It showed that while people believe facial expressions are most important, body language was actually a better indicator of another person's emotional state. In the study, when participants were shown photos of a person experiencing an intense emotion, those who saw only the face guessed the emotion correctly 50 percent of the time. Those who saw face and body together or only the body had a far higher accuracy rate.[6]

Eye contact is another area that gets muddled by friendly advice and common wisdom. As kids, we're told to make sustained eye contact. Early in our careers, we get the message to "look them in the eye" when we talk to show conviction. Public speakers worry about making demonstrable eye contact across a large room.

With the rise of global business, many of us have seen that eye contact is culturally dependent. What's assertive in one country may be aggressive in another. Further, even sustained eye contact in the U.S. isn't what we think it is. When we're speaking, it's natural and comfortable to make eye contact, look away to think, come back to eye contact and look away again.[7] When talking, we build a strong connection by making eye contact about 60 percent of the time, with each steady gaze lasting about seven to ten seconds. When we're listening, we tend to make eye contact more of the time. But when we maintain eye contact for too long without breaking, it feels too intense (or even creepy). There's absolutely a difference between sustained eye contact and the lack of eye contact that smacks of lack of confidence or evasiveness. But eye contact needn't be an endurance test.

Even sustained eye contact isn't actually sustained longer than a few seconds.

What does all this mean? Should we just give up even trying to manage our nonverbal communications because we'll probably get it wrong anyway? No, not exactly. Just be aware that there's no simple answer or quick fix. We assess nonverbals in clusters, often without even knowing why—and we're overconfident about what we can pick up, and from which sources. So, if you've been hyperfocused on one aspect of your body language, like gestures, don't expect it to be a panacea because it's just one part of what people notice. On the other hand, it also isn't as big of a deal as you might have feared.

If you want to show conviction, instead of picking your nonverbal communication behaviors apart with a scalpel, a better approach is to get your head in the game, and let your body follow the lead.

WHEN YOUR MIND SPEAKS, YOUR BODY LISTENS (AND THE REVERSE)

If you're like me, you grew up with a family member who chided you to stand up straight. My grandmother was forever concerned about my posture, worried what others would think of me—or what I'd think of myself—walking around slouched over trying to make myself smaller. While her nagging was particularly annoying around my tween years, it did result in a certain way of carrying myself as an adult. For that, I'm now thankful.

My grandmother had never heard of the term "embodied cognition," but that's exactly what she was getting at on some level. Not only does our brain impact our body, but our body also impacts our brain. When we stand up straight, we're starting a positive cycle where we feel better about ourselves.

Embodied cognition is the finding that our brain impacts our body, and our body also impacts our brain.

The link between our bodies and how we think and feel (and the reverse) plays directly into displaying conviction and managing nonverbal behavior. If we know the emotion and energy we want to convey, that's more likely to show up in our body language. When we display that emotion and energy, then it confirms our conviction that much more. Sounds like a little bit of hocus pocus, but researchers have proven it empirically.

Harvard Professor Amy Cuddy is well-known for her work on power poses, having delivered a TED Talk and published a book called *Presence*. Cuddy and her Harvard colleagues performed a study examining how powerful and powerless poses affect our bodies and minds.[8] Powerful poses are large and take up space, such as standing with legs apart and hands on hips or spreading out in a chair. Powerless poses are when we make ourselves small, such as when we cross our arms and legs, or when we hunch over. The researchers found that when participants made powerful poses for a few minutes, their testosterone levels went up and cortisol levels (stress hormones) went down. Powerless poses had the opposite effect.

Cuddy's intriguing study brings a physiological element to what had been studied as a mental effect. It will undoubtedly be studied further. A 2015 study set out to confirm Harvard's findings, but couldn't replicate the chemical changes. However, the study did find that people *felt* more powerful in powerful poses.[9]

Other studies have similarly shown how our bodies affect our feelings around confidence, power, and influence. Posture is an area with a heavy mind-body correlation. A 2009 study published in the *European Journal of Social Psychology* looked at how our posture impacts our self-confidence.[10] The researchers had participants assume erect or slumped over postures, fill out mock job applications, then rate their strength as candidates. The study showed that posture had a significant effect on these ratings. Sitting slumped over was associated with lower work-related self-confidence than sitting straight up.

Even when people simply describe powerful people, posture is a key part of it. Participants in research studies have described powerful people as having an erect posture and forward lean.[11]

Posture is one area of nonverbal communication most closely correlated with power and influence.

Adam Galinksy at Columbia University is a recognized expert in how hierarchy and power impacts thinking and behavior. Discussing his work in *Scientific American*, Galinksy writes: "Not only does power change the body, but altering one's posture changes one's power, or at least the psychological experience of it."[12] His research has found that posture is the closest correlate of power-related behaviors. "Only posture affected the implicit activation of power, the taking of action, and the tendency to see the forest for the trees." Galinsky argues that posture is even more indicative of actual influence than one's hierarchical position. If you carry yourself with influence, others will react to you that way.

It's easy to see why you can enhance your show of conviction through a confident posture. After all, both are about assurance. I've previously discussed the value of smiling to show openness, and to invite another into the conversation. Though not all Inspire Path conversations are ones to smile about, when they are about positivity, optimism, joy, or excitement, smiling works in more ways than one. In another example of our bodies influencing our minds, studies show that when we smile it elevates our mood. Smiling benefits happiness and physical health, and even helps the heart recover more quickly after stressful events.[13] Not all smiles are equal, however. In real smiles—known as "Duchenne smiles" in research—we smile with the side muscles of our mouths and our eyes too, crinkling them in the corners. Duchenne smiles involve both voluntary and involuntary reactions. We can recognize the difference in others and in ourselves.

We can discern a real smile from a fake one. Smiling produces a range of feel-good benefits.

Where does all of this leave us? I'm the first to admit that it's complicated. Let me sum it up in three ways. First, people desire to know the right way to show up verbally and nonverbally to be most effective. Second, there is no right way: We don't respond to someone's communication style trait by isolated trait. We take them in through a series of aspects that we can't always logically explain. Third, instead of trying to get a checklist of communication attributes to put on like a suit, we're more effective when we consider the nuanced ways that we can put our thoughts in our bodies, and let our bodies confirm our thoughts. Rather than perfection, we should strive for alignment. In this way we can show conviction from our most authentic place.

CONCEPT IN ACTION

GUIDELINES, NOT RULES

To show a passionate conviction, we must speak like we mean what we say. If others can't recognize that we believe what we're saying on a deep and authentic level, they will never take the leap with us. The bigger the mental jump we're asking someone to take, the more conviction we have to present. This doesn't mean that we have to be rigid or controlling. We can still keep an open mind and hold the outcome lightly. We're displaying our conviction so others might catch some for themselves. In this way, it's a passionate invitation.

Because there's so much nuance around communicating conviction, especially the nonverbal components, I'll do my best in this section to boil it all down to what's most consistent and relevant. This includes the most frequent advice I give to clients to help them be convincing and inspiring communicators. I hope that by now you've gotten that I don't believe it's helpful to get overwhelmed with technique. Please don't use this as a checklist! Remember that others read you through a cluster of signals, so rather than hard and fast rules, I'll present guidelines for what you can consider to show up with a clear head, aligned words and body language, and an ability to express conviction around what you're communicating.

TRY ON THE MESSAGE

When we're preparing for a conversation, it's typical to concentrate primarily on what we want to say. As we discussed in Chapter 7, to show passion, we need to connect to the heart of the message, understanding our connection to it. This forces us to stop and get our head and heart in the game. Once we know what's meaningful to us about our message, then we need to ensure that our body supports the words coming out of our mouths.

The first part then, getting underneath the emotion and setting an intention, is a mental reflection exercise. The second part, however, is a physical reflection exercise. To convey the emotion behind the message, it helps to visualize—to see in your mind's eye—what that emotion looks like for you. How does excitement show up in your body? How about gravity? Concern? Joy? Urgency?

If you walk into a conversation crystal clear about what you care about, then it will more easily flow through the rest of your delivery.

This is not about finding a right way. It's not about imitating. It's about sitting with the emotion you want to convey and the message you want to communicate, and considering what that looks like *in action*. Consider it a sort of dress rehearsal. If you need some inspiration, take a look at some of the communicators who you admire and see what they do. But in the end, the answer to this question will be unique to you.

This process doesn't require a significant investment of time. If you walk into the conversation crystal clear on what you care about, and you're able to visualize how to convey it, then it will flow through the rest of your delivery.

SPEAK SIMPLY

In this section we've talked mostly about body language, but what we say and how we say it deserves attention as well. When a conversation carries weight, we can fixate on speaking the right words or getting our sentences just right. We may even bring in fancy words or esoteric data to make ourselves seem smart or validate our arguments. My advice here: Simple is best.

A 2016 Carnegie Mellon analysis of the rhetoric of presidents and presidential candidates found that most speak at a sixth- to eighth-grade level.[14] Lincoln topped the list by speaking at a tenth-grade level. For some this sounds dispiriting—but think of the broad audience presidents need to address and the need to be inclusive. There's an interesting message here for all of us. You can communicate complex ideas using simple terminology. Most business leaders can handle more intellectual rigor, certainly, but everyone likes to be communicated to at a comfortable comprehension level. This allows us to fully get what you say, not to get hung up on words that we don't quite understand or complex concepts that require deliberation while you're already making your next point. Further, using SAT words to show off our vocabularies isn't helping either. Many people throw out big words to appear intelligent, when research indicates that using unnecessarily complex words makes you seem less smart.[15]

Even smart people prefer to be communicated to at a comfortable comprehension level.

Beyond the type of words to use, declarative sentences come across with the most conviction.

- We will see more global innovation in the next year than in the past decade.
- You can change your team's culture.
- I stand by the sales projections.

This is in contrast to the qualified language that all too often waters down our statements. It can be as common as prefacing our main points with "I think." (If you're speaking, we already know it's what you think.) We also insert caveats that we hope will offer more explanation or give us a buffer. One of the effects of thinking so much faster than we talk is that we think of caveats on the fly. When we do this and speak them aloud, it makes our speech sound rambling and hard to follow. It also makes us sound uncertain. Qualified language sounds like this:

- I think we might see more innovation this year than in most of the previous decade.
- You can change your team's culture if you are able to hire the right people to join the company. Of course, that all depends on how the hiring market looks this year, and if we can talk leadership into more competitive salaries.
- Our sales numbers are solid, but I just realized that you're probably concerned given what happened with last year's projections when Jonathan had my position. I still feel they're correct.

Beyond speaking declaratively, we also show conviction by talking slowly and using an energetic tone of voice. When we're speaking one-on-one or with a small group, it's easier to use vocal variety and to sound conversational because we're in an actual conversation. When we're speaking to a large group, we can lose the normal ups and downs of vocal inflection that keep speech from sounding monotone. This is where using stories and emotion words can help to instill tonal variation and change up our cadence and tempo. You can also highlight key words in a talk to ensure that you put extra emphasis on the points you care about.

ORIENT YOUR BODY LANGUAGE:
OPEN, UP, AND TOWARD

While the research on body language isn't always consistent, there are findings that keep coming up in research and are worth bearing in mind. If you are trying to inspire, then you need to get people to take a step toward you. Therefore, your body language should be inviting. To show conviction, we need to display confidence and commitment. Luckily, there is great alignment among how to project all of these. Body language that supports openness and confidence looks like this:

- Keeping yourself **open**: Standing with hands at sides and not crossed, using natural gestures that support your points, keeping a stance with legs at hip width apart, sitting with arms at sides rather than in front of you.
- Holding posture **up**: Shoulders back and not hunched over, posture straight yet not rigid, balanced and centered without leaning toward one side or weighted on one hip.
- Coming **toward** the other party: Leaning toward another rather than away, stepping out from behind a lectern or desk, walking into an audience, and turning your midsection (not just your face) to the other parties you're addressing.

Now this may seem like a lot to remember when you're trying to be authentic and present and all the other things I've suggested. Just remember the acronym OUT: Open, Up, and Toward. You'll hit most of what you need to show conviction and increase your resonance through body language.

For body language, just remember OUT: Open, Up, and Toward. This hits most of what you need to show conviction.

Now, here's an even quicker shortcut: learn to manage your default posture. We all have a go-to way of standing and sitting. We're in this natural position most of the time. If you don't know what your default posture is, ask someone to observe you or try to observe yourself. Are you Open, Up, and Toward? If not, try to correct it when you can. For example, my default is to cross my arms. This is not an inspiring stance, and definitely gets in the way of my desire to show up in an open way as a coach! When I notice myself crossing my arms, I gently move them to my side or on armrests of a chair. It doesn't take a ton of preparation or even recognition to get to a more aligned body orientation.

SMILE. UNLESS YOU SHOULDN'T

I've said it before, and there's not much more to say than the obvious: Smile early and often, unless it's inappropriate to your message. Of course there are times when the occasion would be grossly inappropriate to smile, for example, eliminating someone's position or counseling a grief-stricken team. But for the most part, if you want to inspire more, smile more.

Smile early and often, unless you absolutely can't. (And that's rare.)

Smiling puts both you and the audience at ease. It encourages connection. It relaxes the body, flooding it with good emotions. Especially when nervous or uncomfortable, it's easy to come across as overly serious. (For a fun experiment, watch a video of leaders speaking with the volume turned off to see the message that their body language sends. A speech meant to rally the troops can look like a layoff announcement.) To make your smile real, insert lighthearted asides, jokes, or stories that make you naturally feel good. This way, no faking is needed.

YOU BRING THE WEIGHT TO WHAT YOU SAY

If we care about what we say, and we're relaxed and comfortable, conviction should come through easily. It's when we're playing on uncertain terms, or in new or high-stakes situations, where we start to get in the way of our own message. We may mean what we say, but that meaning gets lost—and with it, the strength of our conviction. Rather than trying to dissect your words or nonverbal communications, think about alignment. Figure out what you care about and how you want to show up to convey that. Then ensure that your whole body underscores that message. Again, don't use the ideas in this chapter as a checklist, but as considerations so you don't get in the way of your message. Only you can bring the weight to your words, and only in your own way.

TAKEAWAYS

FROM CHAPTER 9

⊙ We need to see conviction—it's not enough to read it or hear about it thirdhand. Communicators show conviction through a range of verbal and nonverbal communications.

⊙ People get fixated on individual elements of nonverbal communications, such as gestures or eye contact, but we evaluate others using a cluster of behaviors. These include words, tone, facial expressions, gestures, posture, touch, spatial distance, and appearance.

⊙ We think we're better at reading other people's nonverbal signals than we actually are. Many times, we either get them wrong, or don't know why we get them right.

⊙ To show conviction, instead of focusing on single nonverbal behaviors, focus on aligning your nonverbal with your words, and both with your intent. This helps your body and mind to work together to show up with clarity.

⊙ To speak with more conviction, first try on the message visually, so you can see yourself in action. Then speak simply; orient your body OUT: open, up, and toward; and give a natural smile that shows confidence.

PURPOSEFUL

SPOTLIGHTING
MEANING

CHAPTER 10

PURPOSEFUL CONVERSATIONS

"As far as we can discern, the sole purpose of human existence is to kindle a light in the darkness of mere being." —*Carl Jung*

"A mighty flame followeth a tiny spark." —*Dante*

The human desire to identify and spark a purposeful light in our days is a very real part of our orientation to work—where after all, we spend most of our waking hours. When we have a clear purpose to this time, and our path is illuminated, work is invigorating. We have harmonious passion, or at the least, contentment. When we feel as though we're running in circles, or spiraling downward, work is somewhere between boring and soul crushing. We're counting the hours (or, if nearing retirement, years) until we're free.

Helping clients to get clear about their purpose is a core part of many coaching engagements. Even if that's not the presenting issue, it almost always comes up as it's linked to everything else. If passion is the accelerator, it's purpose that steers the car. Purpose is our driver. It's the reason we want to get better in the first place. Purpose feeds intrinsic motivation. It's what creates meaning from our labor.

Finding an inspired purpose is a question for young professionals as well as seasoned CEOs, for people working in nonprofits and on Wall Street. It's an equal opportunity desire. We all want purpose, even if we don't know where to find it. When we don't have a clear purpose, we feel something is missing. It's hard to capture, and slippery when seized.

Finding an inspired purpose is an equal opportunity desire in every type of job, at every point in our careers.

Consider the case of Brian, who represents a common situation of many mid-career professionals. Brian worked diligently in his career to become partner at his law firm. He put in the sleepless nights, forsaking many evenings at home with his family, and hustled to service clients and bring in new business. He'd never liked the culture of high-pressure billing at law firms, but he played the game and played it well.

Finally, he was in the process to make partner, and all signs were that he was a shoo-in. He wanted to be happy about it, but to his surprise, he was ambivalent. Becoming an equity partner required a substantial financial commitment that made Brian feel trapped. Few partners leave once they make it in. He began to question why he became an attorney in the first place, and where he wanted his path to go from here. He made a gutsy decision and deferred the partner process for a year to fully explore his options. In the end, he left the firm to become in-house counsel for a company whose values aligned with his own, and which allowed him to be part of building an organization.

Another very different example is Nancy, who started her own company filled with purpose to create the kind of business she'd always dreamed about. She hired great people, built an energizing culture, and worked with forward-thinking clients. Nancy ran the company with a "no jerks" policy for employees, partners, and customers. Everyone in the company's orbit was respected and respectful. Nancy had never felt so on her game.

Five years in, Nancy took in venture capital to help finance an expansion. The VCs had their own ideas for how Nancy should grow the company, as well as a timeline for an exit. They brought in a hotshot COO to guide the company's growth. Within a year, Nancy's company was making more money than ever, with a new management team as well as additional investors. Nancy, however, was miserable. She barely recognized the company she'd started, and dreaded going into work. She'd lost her entrepreneurial spirit to bring her vision into the world, and felt lost without it.

Nancy tried a few different avenues to get her motivation back, including running a strategic division that specialized in new product development. However, she kept bumping up against a creatively stifling culture that didn't feel like home. Eventually, she worked out an exit agreement and left.

As these two examples highlight, purpose is a personal endeavor. It exists within us, and it may be impacted by the situations in which we find ourselves. We can have it, lose it, and regain it. We may only have a partially formed seed of purpose that either flowers or gets buried, depending on the environment.

We hear a lot about purpose-driven organizations like Starbucks ("to inspire and nurture the human spirit—one person, one cup, and one neighborhood at a time") or Nike ("to bring inspiration and innovation to every athlete in the world").[1] And yes, it can be inspiring to work for an organization with such a clear sense of purpose—especially when that purpose aligns with your own. On the other hand, if there's an explicit or implied corporate purpose that conflicts with your values, it can make you miserable.

But for most people, the process of finding purpose exists on a more nuanced, personal scale. It's less about a grand vision outside of ourselves and more about the vision we possess internally. Those who inspire us know this. That's why they're willing to have conversations about purpose, even pointing to it when we're not looking for it. Helping someone find that internal spark of purpose, or reignite it, is a transformational act. Inspire Path conversations around purpose may occur in front of a room full of people, helping them to see a higher calling for their work. Or they can be one-on-one, helping another person to kindle that light to want to be, and do, more.

A purpose that ignites us is personal. It's less about a vision outside of us, and more about the vision we possess inside.

PURPOSE: BIG, SMALL, AND IN THE MIDDLE

We can engage in Inspire Path conversations about purpose pretty much anytime. We're so often in these conversations inside our own minds, that when someone else goes there with us, it's appreciated. You may be thinking that it's awkward to go up to your colleague on any given afternoon and start talking about his purpose. Like most Inspire Path conversations, timing matters. You have to have the space to be present, personal, and passionate about the topic. But I would also say that there are many levels to purpose, and each has meaning. You don't have to go nearly as deep as you think.

Purpose can seem grandiose, mostly because we think of it in big terms. This is your life's purpose, the Big P, the grand design for your life, your organizing principles. Many people never figure this one out, but certainly any step closer is positive. It can be hugely motivating to have someone help us in this search, but it's intimidating to enter into this conversation. We often leave the Big P to the professionals—psychologists, coaches, or spiritual leaders. Our family, close friends, and mentors help, too.

On the flip side is the small p purpose—the purpose for what we're doing at the time. This is why the project you're working on feels significant, or why it's important that your research fits into the larger program. Small p purpose brings context and a "why" to our efforts. Even helping to illuminate this basic level of purpose brings empowerment. This is why good team leaders strive to connect daily tasks to a larger company mission. It contextualizes the work, making it about something larger than one person.

In between these types of purpose, there's the middle—which we can aptly call middle p purpose. This is the place where inspired leaders can really have an impact. This middle p purpose is contextual. It's about finding work that's meaningful to us *for where we are at this moment* in our lives and in our careers. It helps to transcend what we're doing in the here and now—to find the patterns that enable us to go further in our journey, to find enhanced enjoyment, to tap into our passion, and to be in service to a larger cause. It's our own personal why: why, given all the choices before us, we are doing what we're doing at this point in time, and why it's important to us.

Leaders can have a great impact in helping another find work that's meaningful for where one is at this moment in one's life and career.

The middle p place offers a practical conversational platform about purpose. I've witnessed people in this area of discussion get a firm handle on a larger why for their efforts, and visibly consolidate their energy behind it. Here are a few examples:

- A leader in a chaotic culture determines she's in the biggest learning situation of her career.
- A manager in a stagnant job realizes his main purpose is maximizing family time with his kids through their teen years.
- A new professional decides she'll use her unfulfilling entry-level job to better figure out her true interests and talents.

- A CEO uses the power of his position to tackle a larger social cause.
- An executive with a controlling boss learns to rise above the negativity to build higher-level relationships to further her career.

In my research, I heard over and over again how particular inspirational conversations had helped to trigger this kind of personal definition. It doesn't have to be a grand life epiphany—but if it is, that's great too. More commonly, it's a personal sense of purpose that enables us to find meaning for where we are, and to feel the pull of momentum carrying us forward.

Simon Sinek, author of *Start with Why*, helps organizations and individuals find purpose.[2] One of his book's themes is that if we don't know why we're doing what we're doing, we won't know how to accomplish our goals. But if we can determine the why, our perspective for how expands dramatically. Further, we find purpose not by starting with the goal and working backward (I want to get promoted because I like a challenge) but by starting with *you* and letting that lead to a goal (I like challenges, so how can that manifest?). All too often, we talk ourselves into a goal without ever having thought through why we want it, as was the case of Brian, in our earlier example, who struggled with wanting to be partner at his law firm.

THE PURPOSE OF PURPOSE

As we've discussed, being inspirational is about creating a space for others to come toward you. It's subtle. It's about establishing conditions for inspiration rather than forcing a preordained plan. After all, we can't make someone be inspired—they have to choose that for themselves.

In the Introduction, I mentioned research by Thrash and Elliot that found three characteristics of an inspirational state: transcendence (an awareness of new or better possibilities), evocation (receptiveness to an influence outside of oneself), and approach motivation (feeling compelled to bring the idea into action).[3] Further, Thrash and Elliot differentiated that we can be inspired *by* something as well as *to* something.

Purpose and inspiration are closely related in the research, and causally related in our own lives.

Having a purpose is inspiring to us, as are those who help us find it. When we are able and willing to be in a purpose conversation, to ask insightful questions, make recommendations, and role model possibilities, we are supporting all three characteristics of inspiration. We act as a trigger for inspiration in others. We're the *by* in someone else's inspiration—and purpose is the *to*.

Being an inspirational force for another may be enough of a reward. We get a big psychic boost from being that helpful. However, there are ample business reasons to support the development of purpose in others. Purpose and inspiration have been shown to increase well-being and goal progression as well as vitality, positivity, and life satisfaction.[4] A study conducted by the firm Imperative and New York University found that purpose-oriented people are more likely to be leaders and to experience work as an opportunity to make an impact. The same study concluded that only 28 percent of the population is purpose-oriented, while 72 percent define work around external factors such as financial gain or status.[5] With that yawning gap, the study's authors argue that there's significant room and benefit to bringing a purpose orientation into the workforce.

Purpose also has a relationship to self-motivation. In their seminal and oft-cited research, psychology scholars Edward Deci and Richard Ryan studied what creates intrinsic motivation.[6] They developed a construct called Self-Determination Theory (SDT), which has been expanded upon by researchers around the world. SDT states that we have three innate needs that, if satisfied, optimize our functioning and growth: competence, autonomy, and relatedness. In other words, we have an inner drive to feel competent and effective, to control the course of our lives, and to have satisfying relationships with others. (Those who've read Dan Pink's bestseller *Drive* will find these similar to Pink's thesis that we're driven by mastery, autonomy, and purpose.) We all have these drives, but they can be supported or stymied by our environments, as well as by our own mindsets.

When we help people tap into their purpose, we are not just inspiring, we are helping them to self-motivate. Purpose-driven conversations tie directly into these drives. We help people to figure out their strengths (competence), how to put them to better use (autonomy), and how to be part of a larger effort (relatedness). Sometimes people need to find all three, or to be reminded of just one, like competence. This is why the simple act of sincere, specific, positive feedback can be inspiring. We're reminding someone of their competency.

When we help people tap into their purpose, we are not just inspiring, we are aiding their intrinsic motivation.

Finally, it's worth noting that being a purpose-driven communicator is less of an event than an orientation. There's no right time or place to have these conversations, which tap into that internal drive toward purpose as an important part of what it means to be a leader, a worker, and a human. What matters most is that both parties are open to having them.

A CASE IN PURPOSE:
GOVERNMENT LEADERS

Though I work primarily with corporate clients, by living and working in the D.C. area, my work occasionally takes me into the world of government. Usually, I'm brought in to deliver a keynote to a federal agency. We all hear the stories of what it's like to work in the government—byzantine rules, tenure-track career paths, and rotating political appointees in leadership. And yet, some of the most dedicated and smartest people I've known have worked in government. In my preparation to learn about the audience, I always ask about the organizational culture, to learn what this specific agency is experiencing, and what it is trying to instill.

Agency culture can vary tremendously. There's a big difference between working at NASA and the Department of Education, for example. Every year, a federal employee job satisfaction survey goes out to all government employees where they rate their agencies on employee engagement and satisfaction. Since its founding in 2003 as a response to 9/11, the Department of Homeland Security (DHS) continually ranks at the bottom of the list of agencies. It's become such a trend in Washington that hearings have been called to discuss why morale at DHS is chronically low.[7]

Knowing some people who've worked at DHS over the years, I've asked about this phenomenon. There have been leadership changes and considerable integration issues from bringing twenty-two separate agencies together to form DHS, and that surely plays a role. But what I hear about most is the thwarting of purpose. There's a disconnect between what the workers at DHS need to do, and what they can do—made even worse by negative public perceptions.[8] Think about it: The mission of DHS is to keep the homeland safe. That means the TSA at airports, the Coast Guard, Border Protection, Immigration, Secret Service, and FEMA, to name a few. DHS covers everything from complex cybersecurity to stopping a runner at our borders.

People often go to DHS from the military or are civilians inspired by the cause. Once they get there, they face an ever more sophisticated and mounting set of threats, and a general public that's vocally frustrated. As I write this, U.S. airlines are encouraging travelers to post pictures of long security lines on social media to ease the backups at airports with the hashtag #IHateTheWait. As you can imagine, the comments are not kind.

Employees at DHS have stressful jobs, with incredibly high stakes—and are continually stymied in their ability to feel competent and to have a sense of control over their work. In fact, it's the opposite: They are in the news regularly for their shortcomings while their budgets get cut, thereby limiting their options. Is it any wonder that so many DHS employees struggle to stay inspired and engaged? Wouldn't you?

It's not just DHS that faces engagement issues in the government. The oft-reviled stereotype of the government worker is a lazy, mediocre employee who is phoning it in until collecting an early and overly generous taxpayer-funded retirement. Again, not the people I've known. (And yes, there are a mix of good and bad employees everywhere.) Washington is a company town. Everyone here knows federal employees. They are Ph.D.s and researchers, economists and genomic scientists, CIA agents, congressional aides, and IRS investigators. They are budget officers, multilingual Foreign Service workers, and busy secretaries like my sister. To solve our hardest national problems, the government needs our best thinking, creativity, and inspiration. With this backdrop, you can see how important instilling a sense of purpose is for government leaders. Many government workers can make more money in the private sector. Some leave for that reason. However, most don't. Known as career employees in Washington-speak, they've been in the trenches through multiple administrations trying to get important work done in some pretty tough circumstances. Feeling, and acting on, a strong sense of purpose is critical.

Brookings Executive Education, part of the influential Brookings Institution think tank, has been developing government leaders since 1957. It was the first organization to offer leadership training to the federal workforce, and is consistently ranked the highest in the industry. Thousands of government leaders have attended development programs through Brookings over the years. I presented at one of its leadership sessions, and was impressed by the creativity and energy of the government leaders in the room. Rather than being saddled with the difficulties of government service, they were enthusiastically exploring its possibilities. When I spoke to the Executive Director of Brookings Executive Education, Mary Ellen Joyce, I learned why. Joyce described a program built on helping government leaders find and share purpose. In an interview, she shared her thoughts.[9] "I'm proud that we've developed a new paradigm of leadership development," she said. "We call it Leading Thinking. Organizations have competency models that are about behaviors. That's not the place to start. We've backed up to emphasize the thinking first. Without linking it all together, you don't have a framework for developing yourself. It starts with a platform of being able to fully articulate your philosophy of living a full and complete life. From there you address your values and understand what's essential to what you are. We help our leaders start with mindsets before moving to behaviors.

"We've heard program participants say things in their feedback such as 'You've made me a better man' and 'This approach is making me the leader I've always wanted to believe in.'

"Our participants are inspired, which in turn, inspires others in their organizations," Joyce said.

Beyond engaging participants to find and align their individual purposes, Brookings also helps leaders tap into their very reason for being in government service in the first place. This may also be their big P purpose, and most certainly their *why*. Joyce discussed how invigorating and inspiring this is for everyone involved in the program.

"When you connect people to their noble purpose, they're more inspired and more inspiring," she told me. "When we're in a room of government leaders, we make the connection that they are part of a larger tapestry. The founders who convened in Philadelphia weren't much different than the government leaders sitting in the room. There's something so ennobling about realizing they are part of what makes this country unique, and that they are part of its history. Participants come back recharged, reenergized, and recommitted to make the Constitution truer. They see that what they do keeps achieving this dream of America."

Brookings Executive Education is leading powerful, personal, purpose-filled conversations in government. If we can engage purpose in our largest institutions, we can do it anywhere! Most organizations have far more latitude than the large and complex federal government. Purpose is a fast track to inspiration, empowerment, and motivation. Every conversation you have where you're pointing toward purpose has the possibility to change perspectives, options, and even lives. And doing it is a straightforward process.

Purpose is a shortcut to get people to a place where they're most inspired, empowered, and motivated.

CONCEPT IN ACTION

HELPING OTHERS FIND PURPOSE

When leaders think of purpose, they often conjure up beautifully crafted mission statements, with persuasive speeches to win hearts and minds so it catches on. But we can't sell someone a purpose, just as we can't push anyone into being inspired. We help someone find purpose by creating a space, and by being in the conversation. By engaging at this place, we act as a guide to find more purpose. Think of yourself as coaching around purpose, rather than managing to it.

In our interview, Wharton professor and bestselling author of *Give and Take* and *Originals* Adam Grant shared his own take on helping others to find purpose. He referred to a body of research in social psychology called "action identification theory," which concludes that there are multiple levels of explanation we can use for any one event, ranging from specific details to abstract thoughts.[10] The more abstract, or higher level, way we are able to view an event, the closer we are to the realm of purpose. Grant explains it this way, using our interview as an example:

Anything you do, you can look at several levels of analysis. I'm speaking, so I'm producing sound and moving lips. At the next level, I'm having a conversation. At the next level, I'm helping you write a book. At the loftiest level, I'm sharing knowledge with an audience. We identify our actions in terms of the process, and at the highest levels we're finding a purpose. It's more motivating to think of work in terms of purpose than process. A lot of what we have to do is process, and it's hard to see the purpose all the time. It's a huge role for leaders to be able to help others connect the dots—to show how one's efforts connect to something that really matters.[11]

There are multiple levels of explanation to any event, ranging from specific details to meaningful thoughts. The higher up the ladder we go, the closer we get to purpose.

We coach others toward purpose by walking them up the ladder of this analysis. We don't need to be directive—and we shouldn't be. We're helping them by guiding their thinking. Again, we're coaching. This is what Brookings is doing with senior government leaders—providing a constructive, inspirational space for them to consider their highest callings for their work, which for some goes right up to the Constitution.

Questions are a perfect way to have purposeful conversations. They invite thinking. They gently expand perspective. But the type of question we ask also matters. We know from decades of research that people find internal motivation, inspiration, and purpose through consistent means—by doing what they're good at and enjoy, feeling useful, being in relationship to others, and having a sense of agency that carries them forward.

Purpose exists at the place where we're doing what we're good at and enjoying it; feeling useful; in relationships with others; and feeling forward momentum.

Figure 10.1 provides a guide for how to engage around purpose. When all five of these elements are in our work, we're at our most purposeful and inspired. While many of us won't find all of them tomorrow, with some guidance, we should be able to move the needle forward and broaden our perspective.

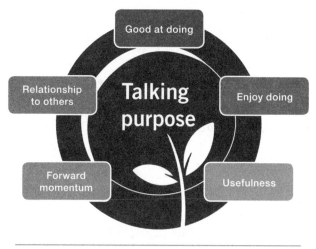

Figure 10.1: How to Engage around Purpose

The rest of this chapter outlines suggestions for how to coach or counsel around each of these areas. They are fairly easy topics to bring up because people enjoy talking about them, at least on some level. In any one conversation, you can hit upon all of them or delve into one at a time.

GOOD AT DOING

When we're doing activities that play to our strengths, we can sense a glide path to purpose. If we feel competent then we feel motivated, which leads us to work harder and with positivity, which only increases our aptitude. This doesn't mean that the activity has to be effortless; it can take a lot out of us. A great musician must work hard to master the toughest compositions.

We all have strengths that, when applied to our work, generate a contented hum as the time passes. If we're lucky, every day we do some work that incorporates our strengths. But in the crush of everything that we have to just get done, it's all too easy to forget what we're good at doing. By leading a conversation around competency, we can help

le others back to this place of strength, and open up new possibil-
; from there.

By leading a conversation around competency, we can
help guide others back to this place of strength, and open
up new possibilities from there.

Questions that guide to what another is good at doing:

- What work activities come easiest to you?
- What do you do as well as or better than anybody in your role?
- What do you take on because you know you're the best person to do it?
- For what actions have you consistently been complimented in your life?

ENJOY DOING

Hopefully we enjoy doing what we're good at. But surprisingly often, this simply isn't the case. A person is good at math so becomes an accountant—yet hates managing debits and credits all day. An engineer is promoted to management, but misses the artistry of product design. You get the point. Many people fall into careers that they're good at doing, but don't enjoy. This is why midlife career crises happen!

When we coach around enjoyment, we're guiding others to a place where they can either find or rekindle what they love about work. Sometimes this leads to the discussion about a career change, but more likely, it doesn't. There are aspects we like and don't like about any position, but it all gets jumbled up in our monolithic J-O-B. We also have way more capability to adapt our duties than we may think. (In my experience, we talk ourselves out of even asking, but when we do, we get much of what we wanted.)

When we coach around enjoyment, we're guiding others to a place where they can either find or rekindle what they love about work.

Questions that guide to what another enjoys doing:

- What are you doing that makes you lose track of time at work?
- If you could design your job any way you'd like, no restrictions, what would you spend your time doing?
- When you consider a high point in your career, what were you doing?
- What would you do even if you didn't get paid to do it?

USEFULNESS

If you've ever been assigned busy work, then you know why usefulness is related to purpose. When we feel that our work is going nowhere, it doesn't matter how much we like it or are good at it; our labors still feel hollow. There's inherent meaningfulness in doing something that's useful—whether to a person, to a company, or to a goal.

There's inherent meaningfulness in doing something useful.

The utility of our work can be obscured due to poor communication, changing corporate agendas, opaque management, or lots of other reasons. At one time or another, most of you have thought, "This is pointless, but I'll do it because my boss asked for it." I've heard this as high up as CEOs delivering information to the board. On the other hand, if we know that our work contributes to something important, we can overlook aspects that may not be ideal. Think of employees who—feeling passionate about the cause—work crazy hours to grow the start-ups where they work. Or stay-at-home parents who believe that raising their kids is their most important work, and sacrifice to do it.

Questions that guide to usefulness of another's work:

- What's most important about what you contribute?
- How does your work help others or a larger cause?
- What's the most critical thing you should be doing now?
- What are the highest priorities for your life and how does your work fit into them?

FORWARD MOMENTUM

Purpose isn't stagnant; it's a movement toward something. Purpose has a direction, and it's forward. It's meaningful to help others move past the current state into a state of purpose that propels them. When people lose a sense of purpose, it's often because they get trapped in the here and now, and can't discern how to tap into the flow to take them to the next place in their lives and/or their careers.

Purpose has a direction, and it's forward.

When we coach to identify forward momentum, we're helping another ideate and create the future state. We're showing how what she's doing today will enhance her tomorrow. We're connecting the dots so he can see why his labor will carry him forward—or to borrow from a prior example, why practicing the difficult music continues to make the musician even better.

Questions that guide to forward momentum:

- How's your work today getting you closer to what you want for yourself?
- What do you hope is possible for you, without setting limitations?
- What could you do next with what you're learning now?
- What do you envision yourself doing in the coming months? In one year? Five years?

RELATIONSHIP TO OTHERS

Finally, in nearly all instances, our purpose isn't a solo act, but involves others. It may mean working as part of a larger team, running a group or a company, being around certain types of colleagues, or acting as a valued contributing voice. We may desire a particular type of manager who supports and guides us. Or the relationships outside of our work may be most important to us: being there for our families or interacting with a larger industry. When we bring the relationships into the conversation about purpose, then we acknowledge the large impact that they have on the meaning of our work.

It's our purpose, but it exists in relationship to others.

The work we do can only be so meaningful. The people we do it for and with matter significantly. We often don't think intentionally about the relationships that support our work, but rather, hope for the best and take what we get. Purpose-driven conversations are precisely the time to get others to think seriously about this key factor to their inspiration and motivation.

Questions that guide to relationships to others:

- What's your ideal work environment?
- Describe your best working relationships.
- How could your relationships enhance your work and broader life?
- What would a culture of your favorite people look like?

PURPOSE IS IDEAL, BUT THERE'S NO IDEAL PURPOSE

Engaging others at the high level of finding purpose may have sounded at first like a formidable undertaking and potentially even a rabbit hole. After all, what if you help people find their purpose, and it's at another company? That is, of course, a possibility. But an even greater possibility is that you ignite a renewed passion for their work at their present company, with a leader (you) who inspired them to think bigger for themselves.

Great leaders do this every day. They continually check in to ensure that what a person does links to what a person wants to be. It's that straightforward. Purpose doesn't have to be about the largest life questions, but can be most effective at its most practical: helping others find meaning in the here and now. When we ask the right questions, we can coach others into finding the right answers for themselves for how to do work they're good at and enjoy, that's worthwhile and moves them forward, and that helps them in the relationships that matter. While we may not be lucky enough to have all of these at the same time, just engaging in the question helps to move each aspect further. What we practice gets stronger.

Purpose doesn't have to be about the largest life questions, but can be most effective at its most practical: helping others find meaning in the here and now.

TAKEAWAYS

FROM CHAPTER 10

⊙ Having an inspired purpose is important to any level of professional. Leaders should learn to engage their people on purpose, which helps to increase well-being and goal progression, as well as vitality, positivity, and life satisfaction. Purpose-oriented people are more likely to be leaders.

⊙ Purpose exists on multiple levels from one's life purpose to the purpose of a discrete work project. An inspiring place for leaders to play is the middle—helping another to determine work that's meaningful for where that person is at this moment in his or her life and career.

⊙ Having a purpose is linked to inspiration and intrinsic motivation. People are inspired by something, and when you engage others in purpose, you create the impetus.

⊙ There are multiple levels of analysis for any situation, from the process ("I'm reading the words on the page") to the purpose ("I'm learning to inspire others"). Engaging in purposeful conversations involves walking people up this ladder of sense-making.

⊙ To guide others toward their purpose, explore what they're good at doing, enjoy doing, find useful, has forward-momentum, and builds relationships to others.

CHAPTER 11

IF YOU'RE NOT WEARING IT, YOU'RE NOT SHARING IT

So there you are, ready to bring out purpose in others, to light their fires.

What are you doing to keep your own fire burning? How do you reignite your own spark?

We spent the last chapter talking about how to inspire others to find their purpose. Here we'll discuss how you, the leader, can keep a purposeful perspective for yourself. This isn't just about pumping yourself up, or ensuring that you have positive energy to share—though that's important. You also need to show, and model, what it means to be a purpose-driven leader, and to live a purpose-driven life. After all, if others can't see the purpose that ignites you, then they won't likely be convinced that you can inspire anyone else. When it comes to purpose, you've got to wear it to share it.

If others can't see the purpose that ignites you, then they won't likely be convinced that you can inspire anyone else.

But let's be flat-out honest: Not everyone is down with this purpose thing. Many people are living their lives, taking it as it comes. Purpose can seem like a luxury—something that blew out with the 2008 recession, or at least with our twenties. Maybe they felt a sense of purpose once, but then lost it and never picked it back up. Or they've adopted a well-earned sense of cynicism. Everywhere they look they see signs that companies are out to make a profit and don't care about employees. Consequently, they're suspicious of any overture involving such a touchy-feely notion as purpose.

For the past sixteen years Edelman, a global communications-marketing firm, has conducted a Trust Barometer research study to assess how the general population feels about its institutions.[1] In 2016, the firm surveyed 33,000 people across 28 countries, finding that trust in businesses is beginning to rise again after bottoming out during the 2008 recession. The public wants leaders to shift their thinking beyond short-term results to long-term positive impact, and it's responding positively to leaders who are attempting to increase both profits and societal benefit. However, much work has to be done. For those without a college education, trust in institutions is below 50 percent in over 60 percent of the countries surveyed, even as trust is increasing for those with a college education. The trust gap in the U.S. is 20 points between these two groups—exposing a concerning divide, and showing why so many workers feel disenfranchised.

A 2016 Deloitte study of Millennials (currently the largest generation in the workforce) found that the majority believes that businesses have no ambition beyond profit.[2] And they want that to change. Eighty-seven percent say that "the success of a business should be measured in terms of more than just its financial performance." Even as frustration runs high, this same group is driven by a sense of purpose. When asked what influences their decisions at work, personal values/morals was the top response.

AN UPHILL CLIMB,
BUT WORTH THE VIEW

You only have to turn on the news or walk around most offices to hear an outcry of distrust and frustration—from all generations and all kinds of workers. Organizations, they insist, don't care enough about the well-being of employees or making an impact beyond quarterly profits. There's no doubt that the social contract that governed employment in recent generations has changed. And yet, the yearning for more purpose doesn't abate. I do see a glimmer of hope. Companies are cropping up that publicly ascribe to a double bottom line: profits and societal benefit. And they're rewarded for it through customer loyalty and recruiting. There's even a new certification—called a B-Corp—which companies can attain for conducting business in ways that also promote the social good. Businesses like Patagonia, Ben & Jerry's, Method, Kickstarter, and Etsy are among the growing list of designees.

We could be at the cusp of purpose-driven companies growing in importance and relevance. Talking about purpose may become mainstream. While this larger conversation about how institutions envision and instill purpose plays out, there is always the purpose that exists within our own selves. As we've been discussing, we can concentrate on that in any situation—especially if we're in a leadership position where it's critical to model a sense of purpose. We can create our own purpose-driven work, culture, or personal space wherever we are. We start by getting clear about our own purpose, and sharing it with those around us.

Regardless of the larger conversation about corporate purpose, we can create our own purpose-driven work, culture, or personal space wherever we are.

In Chapter 10, I introduced the idea of a contextualized, or "middle p," purpose. For most people, that's the clearest path to tapping into a strong inner drive that feels accessible and practical. It requires us to open our thinking a bit. After all, rarely are we in a position to have everything align: our organization's values, our own values, our career goals, and our desires for our broader lives. If they do align, that's good for you. But most of us will need to see the hidden threads, and pull them together ourselves.

We can find our purpose in the present situation when we mine for the good, and find the threads that connect to our own core values and goals.

As leaders rise through the ranks, one of the primary determinants of success is their ability to manage complexity. They have to live with contradictions and make sense of opposing right answers. Uncertainty abounds while decisionmaking intensifies. There are far fewer either/ or scenarios and more yes/and ones. "*Yes*, the product isn't ready *and* it has to ship next week to satisfy customers." "*Yes*, we have a hiring freeze *and* we have new clients to serve." "*Yes*, our industry changes are coming too fast *and* we must embrace them." The larger decisions are rarely solvable with black or white thinking. It's all in the gray.

The same is true with discovering our own purpose. We're likely to find it in that nuanced gray area. "I can't be promoted here beyond my role *and* I'm going to make this a great career platform." "My organization lacks structure, *and* this allows me to take strategic risks." We can find our purpose in the present situation when we mine for the good, and synch it up with our own core values and goals.

When we share and show a purpose, we inspire others to do the same. Role models are a powerful force in motivation. When you see a friend, colleague, or mentor accomplish something, it makes you feel as if you can do it too. In a recent study of exactly how role models help others to achieve their goals, researchers found that role models serve three distinct functions: acting as behavioral models, representing the possible, and being inspirational.[3] As a behavioral model, role models embody the goals of aspirants, allowing them to learn vicariously and increase their confidence. By representing what's possible, role models show how an aspirant can be like them, not just today, but in a future state. And in terms of being inspirational, role models stimulate ideas for new goals and make them desirable.

Role models act as behavioral models, represent the possible, and bring inspiration.

With something as personally valued, yet rarely discussed, as purpose, you can see why role modeling can play such an outsized part. Simply by knowing your own purpose and putting it out there, you act as a safe catalyst for activating purpose in others. You demonstrate what's possible.

For the past couple of years, I've been part of the faculty for Signature Leaders, a program that gathers elite women leaders from around the globe to help them maximize their potential in work and life. Companies like Cargill, eBay, ADP, Hyatt, Ingersoll Rand, and Kimberly Clark put their most senior and successful women leaders in The Signature Program. These are women at the top of their game, managing large P&L responsibilities and sizable teams from companies around the world. At Signature, they focus on one important thing: their purpose. Signature describes itself this way:

Signature Leaders lead with **purpose**. They have **presence**. They **inspire, motivate,** and **engage** people to be more than successful. They help make others **remarkable**. Great leaders do this by **leading intentionally**. They do it because it's their life, not their job.[4]

I've been involved in many leadership programs in my work, and have seen all kinds of different approaches. Signature stands out. The conversations are some of the deepest I've seen, and the results are striking. Women come out of the program and get promotions, take big risks, change directions, and reduce stress. For many, it's a life-changer.

A large part of Signature's success is the result of role modeling. Highly regarded global brand executives take part in the program as invited guests. Around an intimate room, they tell their own stories with stark frankness. The women in the program, all highly accomplished leaders, also serve as role models for each other—openly sharing their goals, successes, and struggles. They become a tight network.

And all of this happens because of the tireless devotion of Carol Seymour, who founded the Signature Leaders program as a labor of love. Carol's passionate purpose has created a robust, growing organization. She likes to say she's "not inspirational but perspirational."[5] She serves as a role model herself for leading with purpose, as she explains:

> I heard from companies that they weren't getting enough women in senior roles. There was a gap in the marketplace, but I also saw it within the women. What gap did they need filled to have the confidence to move up? In my own career, I've had that opportunity. I knew the impact of surrounding yourself with people who've been there before, and can tell you it's not as hard as you think it is. I created an environment to share wisdom. Wisdom is what you can use and take, and it's inspirational because it's applicable. When we hear others' experiences it makes us better than what we are. I had no idea when I started Signature how much of an impact it would make.

Whether it's Carol, the visiting leaders, or the women in the program, modeling how to lead with purpose is the juice of Signature. That's what makes it so impactful, with lasting consequences. I get fueled whenever I'm there, just by being in the room.

FIRE UP YOUR PURPOSE

If you already have a defined purpose that you keep front and center, you're ahead of the game.

You can skip this next part or use it as a refresher. As I mentioned, I'm continually in conversations about purpose with coaching clients. Purpose drives our behavior, and holds great sway over our happiness. When it's missing, we notice. When we lose it, we want it back. We may talk ourselves out of it, but inside most of us want to feel purpose behind our labor and our lives.

We may try to talk ourselves out of it, but inside, people want to feel purpose behind their labor, and their lives.

In the last chapter, I highlighted how to coach others to identify their own purpose. The same questions that work on others, work on us. I've never known anyone who found her purpose while surfing the Internet, sending an email, or half-listening to a conference call. You need the mental space to reflect. Find the time to consider the questions for yourself. If it's helpful, bounce ideas off your colleagues or trusted friends. Find role models who can help you expand your thinking. Go away by yourself for a day or a week. Put the threads together to understand what you're good at doing and enjoy doing, what feels useful, what creates forward momentum and puts you in relationship to others in a way that you desire. This is your base. Knowing it creates a core strength that has genuine meaning for yourself and others.

Identifying purpose is, for many, the easy part. After you discover what motivates you, you need to foster and sustain it. Leading with purpose, or living a purposeful life, isn't a one-and-done proposition. It's about living into that purpose, so it grows stronger, adapts, and enlarges. Modeling purpose isn't about simply stating what your purpose is, but showing it through your actions.

> Identifying purpose can be the easy part. After you discover what motivates you, then you need to foster and sustain it.

For the rest of this chapter, I'm going to share the insider strategies that I provide to my clients around how to live into their own purpose. I'm providing it here so that you can better strengthen your own purpose, and exemplify the impact to others. However, you could also use these strategies to coach others around strengthening *their* purpose. Either way, everyone comes out with a clearer orientation toward what inspires and motivates them.

CONCEPT IN ACTION

BRING YOUR
PERSONAL PRESENCE BRAND ALIVE

If you're seeking greater purpose in your work (and life) it takes focused attention, like anything else you want to strengthen. To use a metaphor that's familiar to most of us, it's not enough to say you want to shed ten pounds; you have to get up every day and make healthier choices. Yes, finding your purpose is critical. You've got to do that first. To make the purpose real, you have to set up your life to continually step into it. Here's what I've found that's helpful.

> To make the purpose real, you have to set up your life to continually step into it.

In Chapter 4, I introduced the exercise for developing our personal presence brand. It's a potent tool to understand and stay in touch with our values. It also helps us to center, and make better decisions. And here's one more use: A personal presence brand lines us up to our purpose.

I advise clients to keep their personal presence brand alive, not to hold it as a static description on a piece of paper that's tucked away. Keep it visible by having it posted on a desk or screen saver. Have it inscribed on a paperweight or meaningful object. Make a point to share your brand with others, so they understand where you're coming from, and are inspired to take a similar approach.

You can model how to use a personal presence brand as an anchor. You can demonstrate what you want to show up to be and stand for in times of stress, distraction, tedium, or frustration.

CARVE OUT REFLECTION TIME

In the rush of getting the work of our jobs and lives done, we barely have time to breathe, let alone think. As we discussed Chapters 1 and 2, we've established a pace where we're rarely fully present and too often are overwhelmed. And yet, to be purposeful, we need time to reflect. We can't phone in purpose. We can't punt on our values. We can't fit in finding our true north between meetings.

You can try a strategy I have clients undertake: schedule a monthly meeting with yourself. Rather than taking whatever time is left over—like Friday afternoon—take the prime real estate when you're fresh and energetic. You can do this for yourself by looking at your calendar and determining when you would schedule your most important work. Then block off at least an hour during that time, to as much as a half day (I know, that's a stretch for most) to concentrate on you. Use the time to pull out your purpose, upgrade it, or change it. See how it meshes with your current situation. Set goals for yourself to engage your purpose more fully. Audit what you're doing now against what you set out to do. Think through some of the larger issues that you never get to address about your career and your life.

Schedule a monthly meeting with yourself to reflect on your purpose. Pick the time when you're freshest, not the leftover space.

Now I realize that this may sound decadent, but in the course of a year, that's twelve hours devoted to your motivation and well-being. Twelve hours! That's nothing! The number of working hours in a year for a full-time employee is at *minimum*, 2,080. So don't feel bad doubling or tripling your reflection time. Shut your office door, go to a coffee shop, reserve a conference room, or sit on your couch during a work-from-home day. But take the time.

Many people find it helpful to have an agenda for this strategic meeting. If you're disciplined about keeping the time held, then also be diligent about making a list of what you need to process during that time. Personally, I take out my yearly goals to see how I'm measuring up, and revise if necessary. Each year, I also set a purpose. And during those meetings I hold myself to account for how I'm living into that purpose. The time is yours; you can make it about whatever you want. I've found that when clients reserve that time and use it well, they begin making choices that align with their purpose and values. With mental space, the fog clears.

FIND YOUR OWN ROLE MODELS

Just as you can be a role model to inspire purpose in others, you can also benefit from role models to keep your own purpose alive and thriving. I've worked with many leaders who go all out for their teams, colleagues, and companies—and leave themselves depleted. As I was writing this chapter, I spoke with yet another leader who was described by a subordinate as "one of the most generous people I've known" and then followed up by, "but I worry he can't sustain this pace without breaking."

We all benefit from role models to keep our purpose alive and thriving. Consider putting together your own personal board of advisors.

We all need external triggers for inspiration, and other people are a prime source. As mentioned earlier in this chapter, role models show us what's possible for ourselves, increasing our confidence and sense of agency. Unfortunately, role models don't usually fall into our laps. We have to find them.

One way to approach this is to think up your own "personal board of advisors." Who would you want to be on it? Who do you look up to? Who lives their lives with similar values to your own? Who exemplifies a future you'd like to have for yourself? Be bold—don't stick to who's comfortable, but push yourself. Who would be truly motivating to be around? Invest in getting to know them better. Take them to lunch occasionally. Invite them out for a drink after work, or simply pop into their offices from time to time. Find ways to be around motivating people. It need not be formal. Simply putting yourself in their orbit will expand your thinking.

WIDEN YOUR APERTURE

No one's purpose stays static throughout life. What lights us up one year may stagnate us the next. We need to find ways to continually inspire ourselves with new ideas and perspectives. We benefit from widening our aperture so we can expand the view of our potential. Assembling role models is one noted way to do this, but it's not the only one. There are many methods to inspire ourselves with new information and stimuli—but most require us to get out of our grind, step away from our desks, and experience the world in fresh ways. Beware the path of least resistance. Its pull is strong, and rarely helpful.

Start reading information that inspires you, that points you toward purpose. Subscribe to a leadership magazine, follow a forward thinker on social media, join a book club or read poetry. Get to an in-person leadership seminar, or find a program like the one from Signature Leaders to engage in a larger community. Hire a coach if you can. Many companies will pay for it. If yours does not, you may be able to find a pay-as-you-go option. Also, new coaches are sometimes willing to discount their prices to gain coaching hours for certification.

Maybe none of that appeals to you—then figure out what does. The more that you can put yourself in places to learn and grow, the greater your chances of being inspired by what's around you. You can find new avenues to ignite and expand your purpose, which in turn inspires others to do the same. It's a ripple effect.

The more that you can put yourself in places to learn and grow, the greater your chances of being inspired by what's around you.

TAKE RISKS TOWARD PURPOSE

It's never easy to take risks. As we age and have more to lose, it gets even harder. We can find ourselves with too much work history to give up, and too little flexibility in our lives to sustain a change. Not all risks are equal. There's the shaking-it-all-up kind of risk, like going from being an accountant to a real estate agent, which is high risk and potentially high reward (assuming you love real estate). And there are the more gradual risks that present themselves as opportunities we either grab or demur. Deciding to change companies, go for a promotion, take an overseas assignment, or expand our role.

There's a time and a place for either of these types of risks. I've seen people make big, brave moves and I've seen them take smaller risks that didn't go as intended. Mostly, I've seen that people are happiest and surest about taking risks—no matter where they lead—when the risks are toward their purpose. Purpose can become a guide or even a litmus test to determine: Is this risk the right move for me? Is it worth it?

People are happiest and surest about taking risks—no matter where they lead—when they take risks toward their purpose.

If we refer back to the last chapter, and the questions to uncover purpose, these can also be good ones to ask when you're considering whether a risk is the right one:

- Does it bring more work that you're good at doing and enjoy doing?
- Can you see how your work will be useful?
- Will it carry you forward in your career and/or life?
- Will you be in relationships with people you'd like to be around, in a way that fits you?

These can give you a start, but as we well know, you might not know the answers until you've taken the risk. That's why it's especially helpful to know your purpose. Now you'll have one more measure to help determine which way to go. If your purpose is to grow and develop, then that opens up one set of opportunities. If your purpose is to optimize your time with family, then that presents an entirely different set of options.

More often than not, we make our best choices when we let purpose be our guide. By doing this, and communicating why we make the choices we make, we reveal our values. This, in turn, motivates others.

PUT YOUR OXYGEN MASK ON FIRST

It's no exaggeration to say that helping others find and tap into their purpose is a wonderful, inspiring act. If you're that kind of leader or person, you will be changing people's lives for the better.

However, you also have to feed your own sense of purpose. Too often, we overlook our own needs to refresh and adapt our purpose, and to intentionally make choices to live into it. Fortunately, if you're already in conversations about purpose with others, you can just as easily be in conversations with yourself.

Too often, we overlook our own needs to refresh and adapt our purpose, and to intentionally make choices to live into it.

When you carve out a regular time to reflect on your own purpose, find ways to enhance your perspective, and surround yourself with people who inspire you, then you become that much more impactful in the lives of others. You don't just talk about purpose, but you model how to live a purpose-driven life. You show others by the way you move through the world, making choices and taking risks, what it means to rise above the day-to-day and make your life about something more.

TAKEAWAYS

FROM CHAPTER 11

- To inspire purpose in others, we first need to make sure we have a clear sense of purpose of our own. This is easy to neglect in ourselves as we try to motivate others.

- Companies and institutions are spending more time focusing on communicating their own strong sense of purpose beyond growth and profitability. On a personal level, you can work on your own sense of purpose in any situation.

- You need mental space and time to determine your purpose, and to strengthen, adapt, and change it to fit the current circumstances. It takes focused attention to keep your individual purpose alive.

- Strategies for living into your purpose include activating your personal presence brand, which is a shorthand way to access your values, and scheduling strategic time with yourself regularly to gauge your choices against your purpose.

- To continually refresh your sense of purpose, inspire yourself by surrounding yourself with a personal board of advisors as role models, and by taking risks toward your purpose.

CHAPTER 12

THE CALL FOR COURAGE

E very day, I'm out there speaking to leadership development executives and hearing about the behaviors leaders need to move their companies forward. Leadership development professionals have the tough job of aligning the company's goals with the skills that leaders must develop to be successful at those goals. It's not enough to roll out a corporate plan to innovate, for example. Leaders have to behave in ways that drive innovation.

Increasingly, courage is a topic in these conversations. I hear how leaders need the wherewithal to make tough calls, have uncomfortable conversations, and exhibit the courage of their convictions. Terms like "leadership courage" or "managerial courage" come up. There's a loud and clear desire—even a hunger—for leaders who can withstand the rigors of the job and show the kind of character that engenders followership.

There's a hunger for more leaders who can withstand the rigors of the job and show the kind of character that engenders followership.

We all want people we can believe in—even more so in times of uncertainty.

As we wrap up this section on purpose, and an entire book on inspiration, courage seems like just the right anchor topic. Many behaviors found in inspiring leadership require courage. Inspiring leaders have to go off the worn path, which takes courage. Inspiring conversations require much more of us intellectually and emotionally. They too take courage. We admire courage in others. We know it's the harder path. We can see the effort required. We get that it takes guts.

Being willing to be in conversations around purpose, both with others and within ourselves, requires us to make courageous choices. Leading a purpose-driven life doesn't happen by accident. We have to make decisions and act in ways that support our purpose. This brings to mind the adage, *if you stand for nothing you'll fall for anything*. While we need openmindedness in our leaders, we don't want to see them act like a reed in the wind. These two concepts work in concert. Opening our minds allows us to determine what really matters. There's a time when standing firm shows others, and even ourselves, what we care about. Our choices bring our purpose in sharp relief.

Our choices bring our purpose in sharp relief.

COURAGE IN ALL ITS FORMS

No matter what kind of organization you work for, it's not hard to conjure up a number of scenarios that take courage. Some jobs are defined by it. Consider leaders driving change or turning a company around. It can feel as if there are battles at every turn—from the culture, the market, investors, or stubborn individuals with heels dug deep.

Courage can seem like a lofty concept, or even a platitude. But it's conveyed by small, everyday choices. Even large courageous moves typically begin as discrete, defined decisions. Think of any major courageous figure in history. Now think of that person's most notable act. You can map that action back to a series of smaller decisions. Rosa Parks became a Civil Rights figure because she made a decision at the end of a long day to refuse to give up her seat. Malala Yousafzai is now bravely inspiring an effort for girls' education, but she first chose to board a bus to attend school, despite the risks.

Now I'm not trying to suggest that to be courageous we have to rise to the level of cultural heroes! But I do want to make the point that courage isn't an abstraction. It's a series of decisions that we believe are right, even if they're tough. These decisions underscore our individual purpose or a greater purpose.

Courage isn't an abstraction. It's a series of decisions that we believe are right, even if they're tough.

Consider a client of mine, a CEO who was relatively new to his position. He was deciding if he should alert his board to a potential risk he'd discovered around product development. At the time, it was only a possibility, and one that he hoped to head off through management changes. The situation didn't rise to the level of fiduciary responsibility that required disclosure. He was still establishing himself, and raising red flags felt like a dicey proposition that could undermine his credibility as a problem solver. In the end, his higher value was around transparency and he decided to give the board a heads-up. The issue never came to pass, but he still believed it was the right move. As he put it, "I needed to be able to look at myself in the mirror."

Courageous actions are rarely comfortable and our instincts may tell us to resist. In fact, courage and comfort are often in direct conflict. An insightful workshop participant once quipped to me, "Just because something is uncomfortable doesn't mean it's wrong. It simply means it's uncomfortable."

It can be helpful to break down the different kinds of courageous behaviors—leadership or otherwise—that we may show. On any given day, we can find opportunities for most of these actions. Bill Treasurer, author of *Courage Goes to Work*, outlines three different types of courage.

- **Try** Courage: the courage to take the initiative, attempt new things, take risks.
- **Trust** Courage: the courage to have faith in others, let go of the need to overly control situations, be open to change.
- **Tell** Courage: the courage to voice concerns, provide tough feedback, assert an unpopular viewpoint, speak truth to power.[1]

As you can see, many of the themes in the book fall within these categories of courage. Certainly deciding to have an Inspire Path conversation can require some serious TRY courage. Hey, just turning off your phone to be completely present can require it!

YOUR LEADERSHIP SHADOW IS SHOWING

In leadership circles, there's a concept called a leadership shadow. It's the idea that the leader's values, style, and actions cast a large shadow of influence on those around him. A leader's shadow can be broad, with influence felt throughout the organization. You could argue that the higher a leader sits, the wider her shadow.

The shadow is something that's more felt than forced. A leader wouldn't say, "Speak like I do." But you see workers adopt the language of their leaders all the time. People within the same organization tend to communicate in a like manner, use the same buzzwords, run meetings and negotiate similarly, and value the same behaviors. We talked about the impact of role models in Chapter 11. Role modeling plays a significant role in setting any organization's culture. And the role models with the greatest influence are, by far, the leaders.

Leaders can eloquently say what they care about, but the shadow is determined more by the choices they make. People throughout the organization are paying attention to what the leader prioritizes: the decisions made, the actions taken, the discussions elevated. All too often, the actions are undertaken haphazardly or accidentally. But when a leader's actions can be made in alignment with her purpose, the message sent is exquisitely clear. The actions are made with conviction, and with eyes wide open.

Leaders can eloquently say what they care about, but the shadow is determined more by the choices they make.

Even the most courageous actions gain certitude the closer they get to our purpose.

SAYING NO AND SAYING YES

In 2015, the outdoor sporting goods retailer REI did something crazy: it closed for Black Friday. Black Friday, the day after Thanksgiving, is one of the most lucrative shopping days of the year for U.S. retailers. We've all seen the videos of people lining up at 3:00 a.m. to elbow one another out of the way as they charge into stores for holiday deals. Black Friday is a critical day for REI, clocking in as one of its ten biggest sales day of the year.

But instead of gearing up, the 12,000 REI employees got the day off, and the stores went dark. The company encouraged its employees to #OptOutside and spend the day outdoors enjoying nature.

"What?" cried retail analysts. This seemed to most retail industry insiders to be a lunatic move. But the President and CEO of REI, Jerry Stritzke, explained it this way: "It's an act where we're really making a very clear statement about a set of values."[2] REI's purpose is to encourage healthy lifestyles. Black Friday, with its growing creep into the Thanksgiving holiday and promotion of mass consumerism, was the opposite.

Stritzke was honest to say that the decision wasn't easy. To a retailer, closing on Black Friday is anathema to good business principles. But Stritzke was clear that this was a decision that the company believed in. REI publicized its decision and encouraged others to join in the #OptOutside movement. REI closed again for Black Friday 2016—and according to several media reports, while #OptOutside cost REI its Black Friday revenues, overall, profits have been up.

This example shows a truism about purpose: we can't have it all. If we want to be for certain things, we will have to say "no" to certain other things. In the case of REI, saying no meant losing a significant revenue opportunity. But it was a way to say yes to the company's—and leadership's—purpose.

This is one reason that purpose and courage are so closely linked. To be purposeful, we need to make courageous choices. We have to say no to some things—like comfort, certainty, and other opportunities. Our purpose is defined as much by what we say no to as what we say yes to.

Our purpose is defined as much by what we say no to as what we say yes to.

Have you ever been offered a job that, while seemingly great from a career standpoint, didn't fit with your larger purpose for yourself? If so, you know how heavy that word *no* can feel to deliver. You realize you are giving something up to get something else. I'm reminded of a client who was on track to become the next CFO of his company. He decided instead to take his career on an operational path, requiring him to decline a promotion in finance in order to take a lateral position in operations to switch functional areas. The decision was hard. It was uncomfortable. It required courage. He was helped, however, by the smaller decisions he'd made in the prior year to test out his operational chops by getting more involved in that side of the business.

But of course, courage can also be about what we say yes to, and how we carry our purpose through our presence. Atif Rafiq is the first Chief Digital Officer (CDO) of McDonald's, and among the first CDOs in the Fortune 500.[3] In joining McDonald's, Atif took on a big mandate: to transform the global giant into a leader in using technology to enhance the customer experience. Atif came to the traditional business of McDonald's from the anything-but-traditional Silicon Valley, with a career built in companies like Amazon, Yahoo, and AOL.

To make such a dramatic move, knowing the passion and fortitude it would take to reinvent how customers interacted with an icon like McDonald's, required a big personal yes. The opportunity felt like a contrarian bet—few would consider a company like McDonald's as a place where technology could become central to growth strategy. Yet that's exactly what Atif believed. Having seen disruptors like Uber and Airbnb demonstrate how quickly the world could change, he could see McDonald's leadership around one of its core value propositions—convenience—being challenged and redefined by trends in mobile, location awareness, and big data.

Atif jumped on board, considering it a "smart risk to blaze a new trail." He explains: "Original thinking requires focus on what will be, not just what things have been."[4]

Once he entered the company, he quickly realized that he needed to apply his deep tech experience to open the sixty-year-old company to new ways to say *yes*—even to things no one had even imagined. Embracing this role, Atif showed others what he knew to be possible. To do this, he needed to believe in his purpose so greatly, even when met with resistance, that he embodied change.

Atif began by encouraging new thinking, supplementing his team with digital natives who had a bias for action and a "why not?" perspective. He structured his team to move quickly. Intentionally using his presence to embody change, even in small ways, Atif dressed in jeans, and asked his team to do the same, eventually helping to incite a companywide relaxation of the dress code.

When Apple was preparing to release Apple Pay, the McDonald's digital team spearheaded an effort to be founding partners, bringing various groups together within days to finalize details. Atif and his team were just getting started, driving exploration of everything from drones to virtual reality. At SXSW, the annual gathering that highlights the newest and hippest of entertainment, interactive media and film, McDonald's made a big splash showcasing a virtual reality–based Happy Meal experience.

At every opportunity, Atif showed McDonald's how technology would enhance the business, putting tools into the hands of decision-makers to expand their view of the sheer possibilities of digital. He did this all with a clear guiding purpose, describing it this way: "I look at my job as an instigator of new thinking, because that's where all new actions begin. It's easy to say something can't be done, especially at a large company like McDonald's. My job is to produce a customer experience that's more convenient and fun than anyone had thought possible. I have to believe in this purpose—and show that belief—in every interaction."[5]

Whatever courageous actions we take—saying yes, no, or staying put—we shouldn't forget that what might feel like a solitary decision to us can impact others. We might not know we're inspiring at the time when we're doing it. Remember mood contagion: We are transmitting energy that others are tuning into. Eyes are watching. If we're in a leadership position, lots of eyes. We're revealing data about our own purpose, and inspiring others to consider their own.

We might not know we're inspiring at the time we're doing it. Remember mood contagion: We are transmitting energy that others are tuning into.

There's a quirky, grainy smartphone video on the Internet that made the rounds a few years ago. It's of a single guy dancing at an outdoor music festival. He's dancing alone, eyes closed, entranced, and looks a bit crazy or at least aided by serious pharmacology. You can hear people laughing at him in the background. Then another person joins him, and then a couple more. Finally, he's dancing with the crowd, all sharing the moment, freely enjoying the music. That one crazy guy inspired a movement.

This is what inspirational courage can feel like. Someone makes a decision based on individual purpose, and takes a bold move, even if it's hard. Others see it. Inspiration catches. One leader's shadow provides room for many people to, so to speak, join the dance.

CONCEPT IN ACTION

COURAGE TO HAVE
HONEST CONVERSATIONS

Situational and experiential courage is a complex topic to turn into actionable behaviors. In this section, rather than offer a courage prescription, I'll outline the courageous moves that come up repeatedly in coaching conversations, in feedback sessions for leaders, and in discussions with companies about core competencies they want to develop. My guess is they will be similar to what you've experienced because they are nearly universal. Are these courageous moves you would like to see more of in your leaders—professional, community, political? How about in yourself?

Few of us like to have difficult conversations. They require so much more of us than the typical banter that drives our days: "How are you?"

"Fine." Yet, we yearn for them across many settings in our lives. As we discussed in Chapter 1, we are hungry for honest, straightforward connection. That can only happen in conversation, when we're saying what we mean.

Leaders who don't have honest conversations wreak havoc on those around them. Conflicts go unaddressed. Problems fester. Disenchantment sets in. I hear frequent laments about how a leader can't handle conflict. When I press further, it usually comes down to an unwillingness to have honest conversations. Many people would rather spend months plotting a passive-aggressive counteroffensive than having one straightforward discussion.

People will spend months plotting a passive-aggressive counteroffensive to avoid one difficult conversation.

When we have honest conversations, whether to inspire, guide, or reprimand, we show that courageous communication is prioritized. We encourage open talk around us, where support, candor, and productive disagreement are valued. We role model how to push through personal discomfort for a greater benefit.

COURAGE TO PRIORITIZE PURPOSE

There's a growing movement within organizations to be more than a place to labor for eight or more hours each day. This is deeper and more meaningful than the 2000s-era concept of providing catered meals and Foosball tables to make work seem less like work. People want their work to have personal meaning, and younger workers especially have shown that they are willing to move around to find it.

We see it in the fact that every large company now has a sustainability executive. Talent development staffs are building programs that address the whole person. After a loud public discussion around work/life balance, we've moved into one about growth and well-being.

In too many companies, however, there's more talking than doing. Workers need their leaders to show how to prioritize their own sense of purpose. They want to see courageous moves from those at the top. When Facebook COO Sheryl Sandberg announced that she was leaving at 5:00 p.m. every day to have dinner with her family, she was overwhelmed by the gratitude of others who valued her openly displayed priorities. I've heard many parents, outside of Facebook and in very traditional industries, say that Sandberg's outspokenness has empowered them to do the same.

Workers need their leaders to show how to prioritize their own sense of purpose. They want to see courageous moves from those at the top.

When we see people around us openly prioritizing their higher callings in their lives, their careers, or their passions, it opens our own minds about what's possible for ourselves.

COURAGE TO BE REAL

As we've discussed, people have an intense desire to know their leaders on a personal level. We are comforted when we're addressed as real people, in an authentic manner. Companies set up various methods to make leaders feel more accessible—blogs, video chats, town hall meetings, and social media accounts. But what really makes the message land is how real the leader is when speaking.

Companies invest in lots of communication vehicles to show a leader's relatability but what makes the message land is how real the leader is when speaking.

There are opportunities for all of us, every day, to choose to be real or not. When we admit our mistakes, show vulnerability, use emotion, or talk to others from the heart, we're making that choice. Inspire Path conversations require authenticity. And authenticity takes courage.

People want less artifice and watertight polish. The more of ourselves we can show, the greater our chance of connecting.

COURAGE TO LEAD BY VALUES

I'll often hear a frustration that workers don't know what their leader stands for. She seems to be subject to board whims, or takes the path of least resistance. Some people lament that a leader appeases so many divergent personalities that it's impossible to know what's real and what's spin. Many workers have been numbed by years spent in organizations that prioritize financial results over any other measure, and they view themselves as dispensable cogs.

On the other hand, I've seen value-driven leaders create a bubble of inspiration in the toughest companies. In touch with their own purpose and values, they are willing to have the hard conversations and make the tough calls. People always know what they stand for—even if they disagree. These leaders' values are the true north to which others align.

Leaders who are driven by values can create a bubble of inspiration in even the toughest of companies.

Being this kind of leader requires the courage to understand what our values are. (Determining a Personal Presence Brand using the exercise in Chapter 4 is a good start.) But much harder, we need the guts to share them and act according to them. What we state aloud grows more real and actionable. We become accountable. I once worked with a leader who started each job by putting his top personal values up for his team so everyone knew them. Then he encouraged everyone to call him out any time he acted against those values. Talk about courage.

COURAGE TO JUMP

Remember VUCA from this book's introduction? We live in Volatile, Uncertain, Complex, Ambiguous times. Movement is imperative. Some leaders are adept at bobbing and weaving with agility, while others—fearful that any move will be wrong—have a rough time changing. Organizations crave leaders who have the courage to take risks, even when they aren't 100 percent sure of the outcome. Yet, this may go against our very nature. We've learned to limit our risk to ensure success. That's why courage is required.

Organizations crave leaders who have the courage to take risks, even when they aren't 100 percent sure of the outcome.

One situation I see all the time: Everyone around the leader knows that a jump is required. They are waiting, waiting, waiting—dying for any change that will take the organization forward. The stasis is deadening. Eventually, the executive team peters out, one by one, all because the CEO won't make a bold step that moves the organization ahead.

Organizations need leaders who can notice their own fear, manage it, and jump anyway.

COURAGE TO LET GO

Finally, we get to the courage to let go. This is related to the trust type of courage mentioned earlier. The work that so many of us do, with loose-knit groups of people across geographies and functions, requires an element of trust. We can guide, but we can't control. We can inspire, but we can't direct.

We could cite many examples of what it looks like to be scared or reluctant to let go. On a tactical level, you see this play out with flexible work arrangements. Many organizations can't make them work because the leaders can't let go of hands-on, in-the-office management. At a strategic level, you can see it with corporate change initiatives. Senior leadership announces the change, but cannot personally let go of business as usual, and so it fails.

Remember, for everything we say yes to, we are letting something else go to make room. That can feel in conflict to our very identity. We may equate letting go with giving up or with a lack of resolve. But don't. Being able to trust, loosen the reins, or totally let go can be the height of bravery.

Being able to let ourselves trust, loosen the reins, or totally let go can be the height of bravery.

THE COURAGE TO WRITE THIS BOOK

Courageous moves can be necessary in some surprising places—even in the midst of positive opportunities. Here's an honest admission: I had to marshal the courage to write this book. I marinated on the idea for years before deciding to put pen to paper, researching and circling around it. After I wrote a proposal and my agent shopped it to publishers, I was still not sure. It took me three days to return my agent's voice mail saying she had good news. The book was literally calling to me but I had to force myself to answer.

More honesty: This book felt risky. It required vulnerability from me. It was different from my last book, which was written with a go-go-go energy that tapped into the popular notion of influence. It would have been easiest and safest to follow that book up with a similar message. But that flew in the face of what I consistently heard was desired and needed from our leaders. The ideas in this book had to venture outside the muscular ideal of a powerful, take-charge professional demeanor. This book needed to be written through a gentler, less transactional lens. I worried that would seem naïvely optimistic when there's so much frustration and cynicism in our workplaces.

And I wrote it anyway.

It took all the types of courage just described: to be in honest conversations, to prioritize purpose, to lead by values, to be real, to jump, and to let go. I don't know what will happen after people read it—only that, like any inspiration, it can't be forced. Some may love it. Others may reject it. I believe that my purpose is to use what I see and hear in service to others. I know that we need more inspiration and that people are craving it within their organizations and in their lives. I hoped to demystify what it takes to be an inspirational person, guiding others along Inspire Path conversations. If I'm able to do that for a few people, then the courage was well spent.

For most of us, this is what courage looks like. We lean toward purpose, one decision at a time. We don't have to inspire legions; we can do it more personally, singularly. We can't know how far our shadow will encourage courageous actions in others. And that's all okay.

We're here, ourselves, with only what we possess.

Yet, we have everything we need.

TAKEAWAYS

FROM CHAPTER 12

⊙ Organizations need leaders to exhibit managerial courage, with the demand increasing with the level of uncertainty and ambiguity in the workplace.

⊙ Courage isn't an abstraction but a series of discrete, smaller choices one makes that build courage. We can use try courage, trust courage, and tell courage.

⊙ A leadership shadow is the subtle influence exerted by the leader's choices, actions, and values.

⊙ Courageous leadership requires clear choices, saying no to some opportunities to be able to say yes to others.

⊙ Courageous moves that are desired from leaders include the courage to have honest conversations, prioritize purpose, be real, lead by values, jump, and let go.

CONCLUSION

YOU'RE ALREADY IN A VIRTUOUS CYCLE

One thing I know for sure: you've inspired more people than you realize.

I'm also certain you'll continue to be a positive force for many others.

I know this partly because you care enough to have read a book like this. Anyone who is actively and meaningfully engaged with others has an impact. To go back to where we began, we often don't know the effect we've had on others when we were simply trying to connect, encourage, and empathize. Only the other person knows the true effect and where it leads. It's as if we're all bouncing off one another in a giant pinball machine. Sometimes the bounce is small, sending us on our way barely touched. Other times, however, we get a big bounce that ricochets off the bumpers—ringing bells and resonating through our lives, changing us in ways we couldn't have predicted.

My hope is for more of the meaningful bounces of inspiration in whatever domains we can get them—at work or in our personal lives, publicly or interpersonally. When we're a force for others to find purpose, when we help them ignite their passion, when we give the gift of our full presence to connect personally, then we are part of a virtuous cycle. We create a ripple effect of positivity, confidence, excitement, agency, and possibility. Who knows where it ends? Maybe it never does.

Inspirational communication—a critical component of leadership—deserves the attention it gets. When you have interpersonal connections at work, you want to do more, be more, and give more. What a stark contrast to work that feels like a grind to be endured.

In these pages I've attempted to break down the behaviors that make inspirational communication more understandable and repeatable. Using research—both my own and that of leading scholars and practitioners—coupled with firsthand experience, I've put together a pathway of sorts. It's certainly not the only way to go about it, but I hope it's a straightforward one.

You may still feel that being inspiring seems too lofty an endeavor. It may seem like grandstanding. That's okay; you can let go of the word. As we've discussed, setting out to inspire might not be the best approach. Instead, try working to create conditions through your own communications that encourage inspiration to happen. Another way to approach it is to concentrate your efforts on connecting in a real and committed way. Let that be your lead, and let the rest follow. Be flexible about the outcome.

IT'S ALWAYS BEEN ABOUT THE CONNECTION

In 1937, Harvard University embarked a research study of 268 men to determine what creates a good life.[1] Called the Harvard Study of Adult Development, it's the longest running and most extensive longitudinal study of mental and physical well-being ever conducted. For more than seventy years, researchers have been collecting data on the participants—regular medical exams, psychological tests, in-person and written questionnaires—to discover how happiness is created and adjusts in our lifetimes. They've looked at circumstances of birth, education, personal and work situations, and how our myriad choices impact us. The study's biggest finding? Happiness comes from the quality of our relationships. This predicts our well-being better than any other factor.

Our human connections make the moments that make our lives. I've never heard anyone describe their best moments at work as times they've sat alone at their desk. Our signature events occur with others. When we reminisce, we bring up stories of our relationships. Our highs are made from those bounces off the people around us.

With a year of solid research behind me, I believe even more strongly than when I began this book project that we can light a fire in others by deliberately choosing to show up and communicate in certain ways. We can decide to take an Inspire Path approach to any conversation by deciding:

- Am I going to be present?
- Will I make this connection personal?
- In what ways can I bring passion?
- How will I spotlight a larger purpose?

The ways we inspire aren't hard; they aren't even complex. We act in this manner all the time, in various aspects of our lives. When we put intention behind our communication, and bring as many of these elements together as we can, then we develop a personal strategy to be a more inspiring leader. We make inspirational communication our default rather than a pleasant accident.

INSPIRING COMMUNICATION ON TUESDAY AT 2:30

Inspirational communication can happen anywhere, of course. In fact, it should! But this is principally a leadership book, so let's end by focusing on the day-to-day of the workplace. It's where we spend most of our time, and frankly, where inspiration is so often lacking. It may feel contrived to think that you can be inspiring at a set time, but really, why not? You can easily be uninspiring on any given day—so certainly the reverse is true!

Think of all the moments in any given work day where inspiring communications would change the entire nature of the exchange. Times when following the Inspire Path could turn ordinary conversations motivating and uplifting. An everyday touch base becomes the best thing that happens in someone's day, month, or year.

This isn't a farfetched notion. It's how inspiration happens. You walk into a situation thinking one way and walk out with a different mindset. Someone, somewhere, is being inspired that way right now. Thousands are, maybe millions.

If you're in a leadership position you have significant capacity to create an engaged, invigorated, inspired environment. You don't even have to be as "on" as you might think. Rather, you can decide to take an Inspire Path approach to routine moments in any workday. Nothing grand required—the moments can be typical, and your contribution modest. Simply adjusting your communication can create a major change. Consider that you're planting inspirational seeds—or lighting small sparks. Imagine the impact you could make if you did it in the following settings.

ONE-TO-ONE MEETINGS

Routine: Most managers attempt to meet with their direct reports regularly in one-to-one meetings. While the effort is commendable, these are rarely engaging. Too often, the manager cancels or cuts the meeting short, showing up distracted and harried. Agenda items are covered in a perfunctory fashion, with many important issues left unsaid.

One-to-ones become a checklist item for all parties, one more thing to pack in during a busy day.

Inspiring: Instead, you, the manager, pause before the meeting, show up present, and hold the space for the conversation to show that you value it. Move out from behind your desk, away from your computer or phone. State an intention for the meeting upfront, and match your energy to support your aim. Hold back any suppositions about the employee to fully understand the situations discussed. Make time to personally connect, listen as much as talk, and keep a focus on the employee's potential. While discussing agenda items, speak authentically and bring in relevant personal examples. Finally, prioritize a set amount of time to check in on the employee's purpose, and on how the current work situation is contributing to his or her larger goals.

GROUP MEETINGS

Routine: Team meetings, status meetings, leadership meetings, brainstorming meetings—it's hard to come up with one that anyone enjoys. No one goes into work to a day filled with back-to-back meetings and thinks "How fun!" Too often, meetings are events to endure, structured with little to no agenda, and prone to rote sharing of information that could just as well be done over email. Participants are regularly checked out and multitasking—which only worsens when meetings are virtual.

Inspiring: There's perhaps no rifer spot for inspiration than internal meetings. The bar is so low that it's pretty easy to soar over it. The first thing you can do is to set a situational intention for the meeting. Know the emotion you want to put into the room before you begin. What kind of energy are you striving for? Share an agenda ahead of time so participants can process their thoughts.

Make sure you're centered and present when you walk in, and encourage everyone to be present by asking participants to voice their objectives before you begin. Ask: "What does everyone want to get out of this meeting?" (If you're comfortable doing so, having everyone start with a couple of deep breaths greatly enhances attentiveness. Sounds like a parody on *The Office* but it works.) Encourage open exchanges and listening, calling out behavior that cuts others off or limits participation. Bring the energy you want to see. Remember, your energy is contagious. If sharing ideas or asking for buy-in, bring a mixture of logic, emotion, and credibility to your messages. Manage your own body language to show openness. Finally, remind the team of the purpose behind any actions that the group determines. Capture the accountabilities, and keep the larger calling front and center.

PRESENTATIONS

Routine: Because we associate public communications with inspirational moments, we tend to think about how to engage and be uplifting when we're in front of people. We prepare more for public speaking than for any other communication event. Some people are more inspiring than others, and do hit that mark. However, you've probably spent enough time listening to dull presentations to know that most have room to ratchet up the inspirational quality. You've got the stage and the audience attention. It's up to you to use it or lose it.

Inspiring: We could throw most of the advice in the book at presentations, but consider three aspects that make a demonstrable impact. First understand with extreme clarity the intention you have for this group of people in front of you. What emotion do you want to bring into the room? If you want it there, you have to bring it. The larger the room, the more you have to show.

Second, mix power with vulnerability. Use stories, personal anecdotes, and plain language to be real. Regardless of the subject, talk to the audience conversationally, as individuals not as a monolith. Never put your content over your connection. Don't overly script yourself, and don't read. Please. (It takes tons of practice to read a teleprompter naturally, and even those who do it well create a barrier with the audience.) Stay open and flexible, and allow any presentation to have some extemporaneous flow to adjust to the audience's needs.

Finally, show passion. Most presentations that fail to connect are delivered by people who lack energy, emotion, and conviction. Match your energy to the situation, which usually means emoting more than in your normal speech. Speak at an energetic pace, using vocal variety. Make an emotional appeal beyond the logic of facts and figures, peppering your speech with emotion words and storytelling. Manage your default posture, and strive to maintain your body language open, up, and toward.

NETWORKING

Routine: Lots of people deplore networking—and even more consider it a necessary evil to endure. The conversations are usually superficial and stilted, with everyone wanting something from each other, but trying to appear as if that's not the case. People look over each other's shoulders to ensure they're hitting all the right people. The whole exercise can seem like uncomfortable self-promotion, where few come away feeling better about themselves or others.

Inspiring: Don't go in looking for anything. Instead—whether your networking events involve strangers, acquaintances, or intimate business lunches—go in trying to give. Be present in each conversation you're having. Put your phone away, focus on one person at a time, and truly connect. In each conversation, spend a majority of your time asking incisive questions and use deep listening. Talk to others about the potential they see for themselves, their careers, and the market. Ask questions that drive toward purpose: "What do you enjoy doing?" "What's most valuable in your work?" "What's next in your career?"

When you share about yourself, instead of a pat, scripted elevator pitch, provide personal anecdotes about your work and what drives you.

People remember not what you said, but how you made them feel. If you can engage people in real, meaningful conversations that inspire them to think and do more, you'll be making strong connections that endure.

DIFFICULT CONVERSATIONS

Routine: Difficult conversations are hard for a reason: they cover topics that make us uncomfortable with people who may also make us uncomfortable. The most common difficult conversation is no conversation, at least not externally. We simply avoid the other person while talking up a storm to ourselves. When we do have tough talks, they come later than they should, and cause plenty of stress. Both parties can leave frustrated and feeling as if neither's voice was heard.

Inspiring: The biggest miss in difficult conversations is that we come loaded with preconceived notions, and proceed only at the text level—never getting to the all-important subtext. Instead, shift your listening to include both the text and the subtext. Don't let the clues go by unnoticed. Call out the nonverbals of the other person. For example, "I sense that you're still uneasy about this, am I getting that right?" Put your own subtext on the table if it frames up the talk.

More important, table your assumptions. Turn the volume down on your internal voice; get and stay curious to what evolves in the room.

Don't assume you know the other person's motivations. Ask. Stay open to the outcome rather than trying to control it. Approach the discussion as a learning situation, with shared observations on both sides. Wait until the end—or even schedule another meeting—to get to action items. Difficult conversations become less stressful if instead of pushing for our idea of resolution we attempt to expand the perspectives of all involved—starting with ourselves.

A SEND-OFF AND A WISH

Being an inspiring communicator is a contribution to the greater good. It's not the well-worn path, and thus takes some bravery, leaps of faith, acceptance of discomfort, and a belief that you're part of a virtuous cycle. It's about showing up in a way that's generous and gracious, but not necessarily the easiest. To borrow from the poet Robert Frost, it's taking the road less traveled that makes all the difference.

It's unrealistic to expect to be in an inspirational mode all the time. Many conversations are brief exchanges, offhand remarks, or concise directives, because that's what the situation requires. However, I hope that this book has expanded your view of where and how you can be inspirational, and the range of impacts you can have. It truly doesn't take as much effort as we might imagine.

There's not, unfortunately, a pat prescription for inspiration. Rather, you must find what works for you. I provided a research-based framework, but it's you who determines what fits for you, and where to apply the concepts. One approach is to pick a concept that you're already good at doing (a core strength), and one that you makes you uncomfortable (a development area). See if you can incorporate more of both into your conversations and notice what happens.

Finally, I'd like to say thank you for reading this book. What gives me the most joy in my work is learning from others, and sharing what I've learned in return. I've expanded my own view of inspirational communication while writing this, and it's changed me for the better. I've passed that on to my clients and friends, and onward it goes.

My wish is that you do the same. Take whatever appeals to you in these pages and put it into practice, even if in a small way. Capture conversations that would otherwise slip by, and use them to give a positive bounce. Make them zing. Inspire because you can. Inspiration can happen any time, and anywhere, started by you.

Be the spark.

APPENDIX

Present
Personal
Passionate
Purposeful

Inspire Path

LEADER'S PREP GUIDE TO INSPIRATIONAL COMMUNICATIONS

BE PRESENT	
Focus your attention	☐ Eliminate distractions ☐ State the importance to you up front ☐ Incorporate conversational pauses ☐ Show receptive body language
Show up centered	☐ Set a situational intention: • How do you want to make this person feel? How do you need to show up to put that feeling in the room? ☐ Take a deep breath before you begin ☐ Reset your energy (change location, take a walk, etc.) ☐ Reflect on a positive to defuse stress
Keep an open mind	☐ Know and preempt where you're likely to jump to conclusions ☐ Ask questions out of curiosity, not to be leading ☐ Detach from the outcome ☐ Say "I don't know" if it's true

BE PERSONAL	
Be authentic	☐ Know your core values and brand ☐ Share cogent leadership stories ☐ State your intentions and be explicitly transparent ☐ Use genuine language and express vulnerability with competency

Call out potential	☐ Tell others the strengths you see in them
	☐ Make a point to sincerely recognize the efforts of others
	☐ Use phrases such as:
	  • I see [this] in you
	  • You're always good at [this].
	  • I'm proud of you for [this].
	  • I've seen how you've grown/progressed.
	  • Let me share what I see is possible for you.

Shift your listening	☐ Listen for the whole person rather than the facts ☐ Listen for text and subtext rather than just for text ☐ Listen for what the other person needs to say and not what you need to hear ☐ Listen out of curiosity rather than to judge

BE PASSIONATE	
Show energy	☐ Understand up front what gives you energy about your message ☐ Know what mood you want to convey ☐ Calibrate your energy to your audience and environment ☐ Emote energy through rate of speech, voice inflection, facial expressions, gestures, and energetic words
Use emotion	☐ Couple emotion with logic to convey your message ☐ Make emotional appeals ☐ Use emotion words that tap into feelings ☐ Tell engaging stories that transport listeners
Express conviction	☐ Make yourself visible (if virtual, use video) ☐ Align your nonverbal with your words, and both with your intent ☐ Speak simply and directly ☐ Orient your body OUT: open, up, and toward

BE PURPOSEFUL	

Talk about purpose	☐ Guide others toward purpose, exploring:
	  • What they're good at doing
	  • What they enjoy doing
	  • What they find useful
	  • What has forward-momentum
	  • What builds relationships to others

Role model purpose	☐ Openly share your own purpose with others ☐ Activate your personal presence brand and schedule time to reconcile actions against it ☐ Prioritize activities and people who inspire you ☐ Take risks toward your purpose
Demonstrate courage	☐ Communicate what you're saying no to and yes to and why ☐ Have honest conversations rather than avoiding conflict ☐ Prioritize purpose and lead by values ☐ Decisively jump and decisively let go

ACKNOWLEDGMENTS

I am honored and grateful that I get to do what I do for a living, and even more, to be able to write about it. So first, I'd like to thank you, the reader, for making this possible. It's been one of the most meaningful experiences of my career to be in this larger conversation about ideas I care deeply about, and to find a passionate community who feels the same. Putting a book into the world feels somewhere between exhilarating and terrifying, and to all of those who've reached out in appreciation, you've fortified me to keep doing what I'm doing.

I am lucky to do a job that never feels like work, and that's because of the people I'm with—lifelong learners who fully engage in growing themselves and others. To my clients, a heartfelt appreciation for bringing me into your confidences, bravely sharing of yourselves, and inviting me along on your leadership journeys. You inspire me constantly.

I'd like to thank my publisher AMACOM for supporting my work for the past eight years, and especially Ellen Kadin, for taking the initial bet on me and doubling down. Thanks to Louis Greenstein for his adept hand at editing, and to Barry Richardson, Irene Majuk, Janine Barlow, and Therese Mausser. The entire AMACOM team has been helpful at every turn with a steady eye on doing what's best over what's expedient—a rarity in the publishing world. I'm lucky to have them in my corner.

Thanks to Jacquie Flynn, my uber agent, who combines just the right mix of support, candor, and push. You helped me get out of my head and on the paper, and made the book better in every way. You've had my best interests at heart, and I'm grateful.

Thank you to the authors, experts, and leaders who shared their time and counsel to make this book stronger: Sigal Barsade, Tony Bingham, Scott Eblin, Sydney Finkelstein, Adam Grant, Mary Ellen Joyce, Atif Rafiq, Carol Seymour, Todd Thrash, and Liz Wiseman. I'm glad to be able to share your messages.

Thanks to the many colleagues and friends who have shared their ideas and wisdom over the last several years about the book's topic and how to make the content most meaningful. I can't list you all here, but please know I remember and I'm grateful. A special shout out to Perry Hooks for her sage advice and wit, and for inspiring me to start the scholarship fund with the book's proceeds.

To my business partners and trusted readers, Mike McGinley and Chris Segall Litvak, a deep appreciation for their astute insights, true friendship, and unceasing ability to make me laugh. And to my colleague Susan Seiger, who can literally make anything happen, all while bursting with positivity. I get to work every day with people I love to be around.

And finally to my family, there aren't enough words or crazy-tight hugs to convey how much you mean to me. You give me the most loving foundation that enables me to grow, take risks, and flourish. To my parents and sister, thank you for believing in me, encouraging me, and just as important, never letting me take myself too seriously. To Smith and Emery, your ability to be who you are in the world with grace and joy inspires me to be and do better. I can't begin to describe the happiness you bring me. And to my husband, Mike, who for twenty-three years and counting has never been less than 100 percent supportive of me: You are, simply, the meaning of home.

NOTES

INTRODUCTION

1. Thrash, Todd M., and Andrew J. Elliot. "Inspiration as a Psychological Construct." *Journal of Personality and Social Psychology* 84, no. 4 (2003): 871–89. Thrash, Todd M., Emil G. Moldovan, Victoria C. Oleynick, and Laura A. Maruskin. "The Psychology of Inspiration." *Social and Personality Psychology Compass* 8, no. 9 (2014): 495-510.
2. Thrash, Todd. Interview with author, May 18, 2016.
3. Ibid.
4. Survey Methodology: This survey was conducted online within the United States by Harris Poll on behalf of The Hedges Company from June 7–9, 2016 among 2,034 U.S. adults ages 18 and older. This online survey is not based on a probability sample and therefore no estimate of theoretical sampling error can be calculated.
5. Bingham, Tony. Email interview with author, July 1, 2016.
6. Grant, Adam M. *Give and Take: A Revolutionary Approach to Success.* New York: Viking, 2013.
7. Adam Grant, interview with author, May 14, 2016.

CHAPTER 1

1. "Item 10: I Have a Best Friend at Work," *Gallup.com*, Gallup Business Journal, May 26, 1999.
2. Fiske, Susan T. "Divided by Status: Upward Envy and Downward Scorn," nih.gov, June 24, 2015.
3. Kleef, Gerben A. Van, Christopher Oveis, Ilmo Van Der Löwe, Aleksandr Luokogan, Jennifer Goetz, and Dacher Keltner. "Power, Distress, and Compassion: Turning a Blind Eye to the Suffering of Others." *Psychological Science* 19, no. 12 (2008): 1315–1322.
4. Dokoupil, Tony. "Is the Internet Making Us Crazy? What the New Research Says," *Newsweek*, July 9, 2012.
5. "Trends in Consumer Mobility Report," Bank of America, 2015.
6. Rainie, L., Zickuhr, K. "Americans' Views on Mobile Etiquette." Pew Research Center. August, 2015.
7. Misra, S., L. Cheng, J. Genevie, and M. Yuan. "The iPhone Effect: The

Quality of In-Person Social Interactions in the Presence of Mobile Devices." *Environment and Behavior* 48, no. 2 (2014): 275–98.

8. Davis, Lauren Cassani. "The Flight From Conversation." *The Atlantic,* October 7, 2015; Price, Michael. "Alone in the Crowd." American Psychological Association, June 2011.

9. Turkle, Sherry. "Connected, but Alone?" TED.com, February 2012. Accessed June 20, 2016. http://www.ted.com/talks/sherry_turkle_alone_together.

10. Savitsky, K., Gilovich, T. "The Illusion of Transparency and the Alleviation of Speech Anxiety." *Journal of Experimental Social Psychology* 39 (2003), 618–625.

CHAPTER 2

1. Eblin, Scott. Personal interview with author, December 11, 2015.

2. Mayo Clinic Staff, "Stress Symptoms: Effects on Your Body and Behavior." Mayoclinic.com. July 19, 2013. Accessed January 8, 2016. http://www .mayoclinic.org/healthy-lifestyle/stress-management/in-depth/ stress-symptoms/art-20050987.

3. Begley, Sharon. "The Science of Making Decisions." *Newsweek.* February 27, 2011. Accessed January 8, 2016. http://www.newsweek.com/science-making-decisions-68627.

4. Capretto, Lisa. "Elizabeth Gilbert: Perfectionism Is 'Just Fear in Really Good Shoes' (VIDEO)." *The Huffington Post.* October 2, 2014. Accessed January 08, 2016. http://www.huffingtonpost.com/2014/10/02/ elizabeth-gilbert-oprah-root-of-every-problem_n_5914412.html).

5. Williamson, Marianne. *A Return to Love: Reflections on the Principles of a Course in Miracles.* New York: HarperCollins, 1992.

6. Frankl, Viktor E. *Man's Search for Meaning.* Boston: Beacon Press, 2006.

7. Argyris, Chris. "Double Loop Learning in Organizations." *Harvard Business Review.* September 01, 1977. Accessed January 08, 2016. https://hbr. org/1977/09/double-loop-learning-in-organizations. ; Argyris, Chris. "Teaching Smart People How to Learn." *Reflections: The SoL Journal* 4, no. 2 (1991): 4–15.

8. Dearborn, Jenny. "How to Live in the Moment and Get Work Done at the Same Time." *Fast Company.* August 29, 2014. Accessed January 08, 2016. https://www.fastcompany.com/3034910/work-smart/how-to-live-in-the-moment-and-get-work-done-at-the-same-time·

9. Cuda, Gretchen. "Just Breathe: Body Has a Built-In Stress Reliever." NPR. December 6, 2010. Accessed January 08, 2016. http://www.npr. org/2010/12/06/131734718/just-breathe-body-has-a-built-in-stress-reliever.

10. Schwartz, Tony. "For Real Productivity, Less Is Truly More." *Harvard Business Review,* May 17, 2010. Accessed January 08, 2016. https://hbr.org/2010/ 05/for-real-productivity-less-is.

CHAPTER 3

1. Ottati, Victor, Erika D. Price, Chase Wilson, and Nathanael Sumaktoyo. "When Self-perceptions of Expertise Increase Closed-minded Cognition: The Earned Dogmatism Effect." *Journal of Experimental Social Psychology*

61 (2015): 131–38. (http://www.sciencedirect.com/science/article/pii/S0022103115001006)

2. Kahneman, Daniel. *Thinking, Fast and Slow*. New York: Farrar, Straus and Giroux, 2011.

3. Ariely, Dan. "The Fallacy of Supply and Demand." In *Predictably Irrational: The Hidden Forces That Shape Our Decisions*, 25–53. New York: Harper, 2008.

4. Ibid.

5. Halvorson, Heidi Grant. *No One Understands You and What to Do About It*. Boston: Harvard Business Review Press, 2015. 47–49.

6. Cialdini, Robert B. *Influence: Science and Practice*. Boston: Allyn and Bacon, 2001.

7. Levitin, Daniel. "How to Stay Calm When You Know You'll Be Stressed." Ted.com. September 2015. Accessed February 02, 2016. https://www.ted.com/talks/daniel_levitin_how_to_stay_calm_when_you_know_you_ll_be_stressed?language=en.

8. Dweck, Carol S. *Mindset*. London: Robinson, 2012.

CHAPTER 4

1. George, Bill. *Authentic Leadership: Rediscovering the Secrets to Creating Lasting Value*. San Francisco: Jossey-Bass, 2003.

2. Gardner, William L., Claudia C. Cogliser, Kelly M. Davis, and Matthew P. Dickens. "Authentic Leadership: A Review of the Literature and Research Agenda." *The Leadership Quarterly* 22, no. 6 (2011): 1120–1145. Wang, Hui; Sui, Yang; Luthans, Fred; Wang, Danni; and Wu, Yanhong, "Impact of Authentic Leadership on Performance: Role of Followers' Positive Psychological Capital and Relational Processes". Management Department Faculty Publications: University of Nebraska-Lincoln, 2014. Paper 123.

3. "Most Admired Man and Woman." Gallup.com. Accessed February 24, 2016. http://www.gallup.com/poll/1678/most-admired-man-woman.aspx.

4. Fry, Richard. "Millennials Surpass Gen Xers as the Largest Generation in U.S. Labor Force." Pew Research Center. May 11, 2015. Accessed February 24, 2016. http://www.pewresearch.org/fact-tank/2015/05/11/millennials-surpass-gen-xers-as-the-largest-generation-in-u-s-labor-force/.

5. Ibarra, Herminia. "The Authenticity Paradox." *Harvard Business Review*. 2015. Accessed February 03, 2016. https://hbr.org/2015/01/the-authenticity-paradox.

6. Ibid.

7. Aronson, Elliott, Ben Willerman, and Joanne Floyd. "The Effect of a Pratfall on Increasing Interpersonal Attractiveness." *Psychonomic Science* 4, no. 6 (June 1966): 227–228.

8. See also the work of Amy Cuddy, Deborah Gruenfeld, and Adam Grant for more on the blending of warmth with competency.

9. Merida, Kevin. "Gore and the Bore Effect." *Washington Post*. June 7, 1999. Accessed February 24, 2016. http://www.washingtonpost.com/wp-srv/politics/campaigns/wh2000/stories/gore060799.htm.

10. Booth, William. "From Stiff to Star: Al Gore's Unlikely Hollywood Story." Spokesman.com. February 25, 2007. Accessed February 24, 2016. http://www.spokesman.com/stories/2007/feb/25/from-stiff-to-star-al-gores-unlikely-hollywood/.

11. Hedges, Kristi. *The Power of Presence: Unlock Your Potential to Influence and Engage Others.* New York: American Management Association, 2012. 18–19.
12. Grant, Adam M. *Give and Take: A Revolutionary Approach to Success.* New York: Viking, 2013.
13. Halvorson, Heidi. *No One Understands You and What to Do About It.* Boston: Harvard Business Review Press, 2015. 11–14.
14. Brooks, Alison Wood, Francesca Gino, and Maurice E. Schweitzer. "Smart People Ask for (My) Advice: Seeking Advice Boosts Perceptions of Competence." *Management Science* 61, no. 6 (2015): 1421–1435. Liljenquist, Katie. "Resolving the Impression Management Dilemma: The Strategic Benefits of Soliciting Others for Advice." Ph.D. diss., Northwestern University, 2010. Accessed February 24, 2016. http://gradworks.umi.com/34/02/3402210.html.
15. "The World's 100 Most Powerful Women." *Forbes.* 2015. Accessed February 26, 2016. http://www.forbes.com/profile/indra-nooyi/.
16. "PepsiCo CEO Indra K. Nooyi Talks Personal and Professional Inspiration During BlogHer '11 Keynote." YouTube. August 29, 2011. Accessed February 26, 2016. https://www.youtube.com/watch?v=7NH3EdYvT4M.
17. George, Bill, Peter Sims, Andrew McLean, and Diana Mayer. "Discovering Your Authentic Leadership." *Harvard Business Review,* February 2007.

CHAPTER 5

1. "JetBlue | Corporate and Social Responsibility." JetBlue.com. Accessed March 03, 2016. https://www.jetblue.com/corporate-social-responsibility/
2. Agence France-Presse. "Volvo Eyes 'No-death' Goal in Its New Cars by 2020." *Industry Week,* December 2012. Accessed April 06, 2016. http://www.industryweek.com/product-development/volvo-eyes-no-death-goal-its-new-cars-2020.
3. Hoffman, Bryce G. *American Icon: Alan Mulally and the Fight to Save Ford Motor Company.* New York: Crown Business, 2012.
4. Rosenthal, Robert, and Lenore Jacobson. *Pygmalion in the Classroom: Teacher Expectation and Pupils' Intellectual Development.* New York: Holt, Rinehart and Winston, 1968.
5. Whiteley, Paul, Thomas Sy, and Stefanie K. Johnson. "Leaders' Conceptions of Followers: Implications for Naturally Occurring Pygmalion Effects." *The Leadership Quarterly* 23, no. 5 (2012): 822–834. doi:10.1016/j.leaqua.2012.03.006. Avolio, Bruce J., Rebecca J. Reichard, Sean T. Hannah, Fred O. Walumbwa, and Adrian Chan. "A Meta-analytic Review of Leadership Impact Research: Experimental and Quasi-experimental Studies." *The Leadership Quarterly* 20, no. 5 (2009): 764–784. doi:10.1016/j.leaqua.2009.06.006.
6. For a succinct overview of research in this area see Livingston, J. Sterling. "Pygmalion in Management." *Harvard Business Review,* January 2003. Accessed March 3, 2016. https://hbr.org/2003/01/pygmalion-in-management.
7. "Gallup Strengths Center." About Clifton StrengthsFinder. Accessed March 03, 2016. https://www.gallupstrengthscenter.com/Home/en-US/About.
8. Finkelstein, Sydney. *Superbosses: How Exceptional Leaders Master the Flow of Talent.* UK: Portfolio Penguin, 2016. Finkelstein, Sydney. "Secrets of Superbosses." *Harvard Business Review,* January/February 2016, 104–107.

9. Finkelstein, Sydney. Interview with author, May 5, 2016.
10. Wiseman, Liz, and Greg McKeown. *Multipliers: How the Best Leaders Make Everyone Smarter.* New York: HarperBusiness, 2010.
11. Wiseman, Liz. Interview with author, May 11, 2016.

CHAPTER 6

1. Goulston, Mark. *Just Listen: Discover the Secret to Getting through to Absolutely Anyone.* New York: American Management Association, 2010. 64.
2. Nichols, Ralph G., and Leonard A. Stevens. *Are You Listening?* New York: McGraw-Hill, 1957. Nichols, Ralph G., and Leonard A. Stevens. "Listening to People." *Harvard Business Review.* 1957. Accessed March 01, 2016. https://hbr.org/1957/09/listening-to-people/ar/1.
3. Haas, J. W., and C. L. Arnold. "An Examination of the Role of Listening in Judgments of Communication Competence in Co-Workers." *Journal of Business Communication* 32, no. 2 (1995): 123–139.
4. Charan, Ram. "The Discipline of Listening." *Harvard Business Review.* June 21, 2012. Accessed March 01, 2016. https://hbr.org/2012/06/the-discipline-of-listening.
5. Bingham, Tony. Email interview with author, July 1, 2016.

CHAPTER 7

1. United States. National Park Service. "Roosevelt and Churchill: A Friendship That Saved The World." National Parks Service. Accessed December 20, 2016. https://www.nps.gov/articles/fdrww2.htm.
2. Neumann, Roland, and Fritz Strack. "'Mood Contagion': The Automatic Transfer of Mood between Persons." *Journal of Personality and Social Psychology* 79, no. 2 (2000): 211–223.
3. Barsade, Sigal G. "The Ripple Effect: Emotional Contagion and Its Influence on Group Behavior." *Administrative Science Quarterly* 47, no. 4 (2002): 644–675.
4. Barsade, Sigal. Interview with author, May 4, 2016.
5. Ibid.
6. Jin, Sirkwoo, Myeong-Gu Seo, and Debra L. Shapiro. "Do Happy Leaders Lead Better? Affective and Attitudinal Antecedents of Transformational Leadership." *The Leadership Quarterly* 27, no. 1 (February 2016): 64–84.
7. Holmes, Jack. "The Dean Scream: An Oral History." *Esquire.* January 29, 2016. Accessed April 15, 2016. http://www.esquire.com/news-politics/a41615/the-dean-scream-oral-history/.
8. Vallerand, Robert J. "Psychology of Well-Being: Theory, Research and Practice." *The Role of Passion in Sustainable Psychological Well-being.* March 21, 2012. Accessed April 15, 2016. http://psywb.springeropen.com/articles/10.1186/2211-1522-2-1. Vallerand, Robert J., Céline Blanchard, Geneviève A. Mageau, Richard Koestner, Catherine Ratelle, Maude Léonard, Marylène Gagné, and Josée Marsolais. "Les Passions De L'âme: On Obsessive and Harmonious Passion." *Journal of Personality and Social Psychology* 85, no. 4 (2003): 756–767. Vallerand, Robert J. *The Psychology of Passion: A Dualistic Model.* New York: Oxford University Press, 2015.

CHAPTER 8

1. Ariely, Dan. *Predictably Irrational: The Hidden Forces That Shape Our Decisions.* New York: Harper, 2008.
2. Haidt, Jonathan. "The Emotional Dog and Its Rational Tail: A Social Intuitionist Approach to Moral Judgment." *Psychological Review* 108, no. 4 (2001): 814–834.
3. Haidt, Jonathan. *The Righteous Mind: Why Good People Are Divided by Politics and Religion.* New York: Pantheon Books, 2012.
4. *Reporter.* Directed by Eric Daniel Metzgar. Featuring Nicholas Kristof. HBO, 2009. Film.
5. Zak, Paul. "Why Your Brain Loves Good Storytelling." *Harvard Business Review.* October 28, 2014. Accessed April 22, 2016. https://hbr.org/2014/10/why-your-brain-loves-good-storytelling/. Paul J. *The Moral Molecule: The Source of Love and Prosperity.* New York: Dutton, 2012.
6. Lin, Pei-Ying, Naomi Sparks Grewal, Christophe Morin, Walter D. Johnson, and Paul J. Zak. "Oxytocin Increases the Influence of Public Service Advertisements." PLoS ONE. February 27, 2013. Accessed April 26, 2016. http://www.ncbi.nlm.nih.gov/pmc/articles/PMC3584120/.
7. Cialdini, Robert B. *Influence: The Psychology of Persuasion.* New York: Collins, 2007.
8. Lindebaum, Dirk, and Deanna Geddes. "The Place and Role of (moral) Anger in Organizational Behavior Studies." *Journal of Organizational Behavior,* 2015.

CHAPTER 9

1. Mehrabian, Albert. *Silent Messages.* Belmont, CA: Wadsworth, 1971.
2. Hedges, Kristi. *The Power of Presence: Unlock Your Potential to Influence and Engage Others.* New York: American Management Association, 2011. 25.
3. Carney, Dana R., Judith A. Hall, and Lavonia Smith LeBeau. "Beliefs About the Nonverbal Expression of Social Power." *Journal of Nonverbal Behavior* 29, no. 2 (2005): 105–123.
4. DeSteno, David. "Who Can You Trust?" *Harvard Business Review.* March 1, 2014. Accessed May 10, 2016. https://hbr.org/2014/03/who-can-you-trust.
5. Ibid.
6. Aviezer, H., Y. Trope, and A. Todorov. "Body Cues, Not Facial Expressions, Discriminate Between Intense Positive and Negative Emotions." *Science* 338, no. 6111 (2012): 1225–1229.
7. Shellenbarger, Sue. "Just Look Me in the Eye Already." *Wall Street Journal.* May 28, 2013. Accessed May 7, 2016. http://www.wsj.com/articles/SB10001424127887324809804578511290822228174.
8. Carney, D. R., A. J. C. Cuddy, and A. J. Yap. "Power Posing: Brief Nonverbal Displays Affect Neuroendocrine Levels and Risk Tolerance." *Psychological Science* 21, no. 10 (2010): 1363–1368.
9. Ranehill, E., A. Dreber, M. Johannesson, S. Leiberg, S. Sul, and R. A. Weber. "Assessing the Robustness of Power Posing: No Effect on Hormones and Risk Tolerance in a Large Sample of Men and Women." *Psychological Science* 26, no. 5 (2015): 653–656.
10. Briñol, Pablo, Richard E. Petty, and Benjamin Wagner. "Body Posture Effects on Self-evaluation: A Self-validation Approach." *European Journal of Social Psychology* 39, no. 6 (2009): 1053–1064.

11. Carney, D. R., A. J. C. Cuddy, and A. J. Yap. "Power Posing: Brief Nonverbal Displays Affect Neuroendocrine Levels and Risk Tolerance." *Psychological Science* 21, no. 10 (2010): 1363–1368.

12. Galinsky, Adam D., and Li44 Huang. "How You Can Become More Powerful by Literally Standing Tall." *Scientific American*. January 4, 2011. Accessed May 10, 2016. http://www.scientificamerican.com/article/how-you-can-become-more-p/.

13. Wenner, Melinda. "Smile! It Could Make You Happier." *Scientific American*. September 1, 2009. Accessed May 10, 2016. http://www.scientificamerican.com/article/smile-it-could-make-you-happier/. Kraft, T. L., and S. D. Pressman. "Grin and Bear It: The Influence of Manipulated Facial Expression on the Stress Response." *Psychological Science* 23, no. 11 (2012): 1372–1378.

14. Schumacher, Elliot, and Maxine Eskenazi. "A Readability Analysis of Campaign Speeches from the 2016 U.S. Presidential Campaign." Eprint ArXiv:1603.05739. March 2016. Accessed May 10, 2016.

15. Oppenheimer, Daniel M. "Consequences of Erudite Vernacular Utilized Irrespective of Necessity: Problems with Using Long Words Needlessly." *Applied Cognitive Psychology* 20, no. 2 (2006): 139–156.

CHAPTER 10

1. Bonchek, Mark. "Purpose Is Good. Shared Purpose Is Better." *Harvard Business Review*. March 14, 2013. Accessed May 27, 2016. https://hbr.org/2013/03/purpose-is-good-shared-purpose·

2. Sinek, Simon. *Start with Why: How Great Leaders Inspire Everyone to Take Action*. New York: Portfolio, 2009.

3. Thrash, Todd M., and Andrew J. Elliot. "Inspiration as a Psychological Construct." *Journal of Personality and Social Psychology* 84, no. 4 (2003): 871–889. Thrash, Todd M., and Andrew J. Elliot. "Inspiration: Core Characteristics, Component Processes, Antecedents, and Function." *Journal of Personality and Social Psychology* 87, no. 6 (2004): 957–973.

4. Hill, Patrick L., Anthony L. Burrow, Jay W. Brandenberger, Daniel K. Lapsley, and Jessica Collado Quaranto. "Collegiate Purpose Orientations and Well-being in Early and Middle Adulthood." *Journal of Applied Developmental Psychology* 31, no. 2 (2010): 173–179. Thrash, Todd M., Emil G. Moldovan, Victoria C. Oleynick, and Laura A. Maruskin. "The Psychology of Inspiration." *Social and Personality Psychology Compass* 8, no. 9 (2014): 495–510. doi:10.1111/spc3.12127.

5. 2015 Workforce Purpose Index by Imperative in partnership with NYU. https://www.imperative.com/index

6. Ryan, Richard M., and Edward L. Deci. "Self-determination Theory and the Facilitation of Intrinsic Motivation, Social Development, and Well-being." *American Psychologist* 55, no. 1 (2000): 68–78.

7. Markon, Jerry. "Homeland Security Ranks Dead Last in Morale—Again—but Jeh Johnson's Morale Is High." *Washington Post*. September 29, 2015. Accessed May 27, 2016. https://www.washingtonpost.com/news/federal-eye/wp/2015/09/29/dhs-disappointed-by-latest-low-morale-scores-vows-to-keep-trying/.

8. For the official record, you can review the task force findings: https://www.

dhs.gov/sites/default/files/publications/DHS-HSAC-Employee-Task-Force-Report-May-2015.pdf

9. Joyce, Mary Ellen. Interview with author, May 4, 2016.
10. Vallacher, Robin R., and Daniel M. Wegner. "Levels of Personal Agency: Individual Variation in Action Identification." *Journal of Personality and Social Psychology* 57, no. 4 (1989): 660–671. doi:10.1037/0022-3514.57.4.660.
11. Grant, Adam. Personal interview with author, May 14, 2016.

CHAPTER 11

1. "2016 EDELMAN TRUST BAROMETER." Edelman.com. Accessed June 07, 2016. http://www.edelman.com/insights/intellectual-propert y/2016-edelman-trust-barometer/. Motivational theory of role modeling
2. "Millennial Survey 2016 | Deloitte | Social Impact, Innovation." Deloitte.com. Accessed June 07, 2016. http://www2.deloitte.com/global/en/pages/about-deloitte/articles/millennialsurvey.html.
3. Morgenroth, Thekla, Michelle K. Ryan, and Kim Peters. "The Motivational Theory of Role Modeling: How Role Models Influence Role Aspirants' Goals." *Review of General Psychology* 19, no. 4 (2015): 465-83.
4. "Signature Leaders." SignatureLeaders.com. Accessed June 07, 2016. http://signatureleaders.com/.
5. Seymour, Carol. Interview with author, March 3, 2016.

CHAPTER 12

1. Treasurer, Bill. *Courage Goes to Work: How to Build Backbones, Boost Performance, and Get Results.* San Francisco: Berrett-Koehler Publishers, 2008.
2. Malcolm, Hadley. "REI Closing on Black Friday for 1st Time in Push to #OptOutside." USA Today.com. November 17, 2015. Accessed July 20, 2016. http://www.usatoday.com/story/money/2015/10/26/rei-closing-on-black-friday-for-first-time-in-its-history/74627872/.
3. Morrison, Maureen. "McDonald's Names Atif Rafiq Its First Chief Digital Officer." *Advertising Age.* October 3, 2013. Accessed July 27, 2016. http://ad-age.com/article/news/mcdonald-s-names-atif-rafiq-chief-digital-officer/24 4556/.
4. Rafiq, Atif. Interview with author, July 27, 2016.
5. Ibid.

CONCLUSION

1. Shenk, Joshua Wolf. "What Makes Us Happy?" *The Atlantic.* June 2009. Accessed June 14, 2016. http://www.theatlantic.com/magazine/archive/2009/06/what-makes-us-happy/307439/.

INDEX

ABOUT THE AUTHOR

Kristi Hedges is a nationally recognized expert in leadership communications, and coaches CEOs and senior executives at leading global companies. Her workshops and keynotes have reached thousands of leaders from the Fortune 50 to the U.S. government to nonprofits. She's also the author of *The Power of Presence.*

Kristi writes about leadership for Forbes.com and is regularly featured in publications such as *The Wall Street Journal, The Financial Times, Entrepreneur, BBC, Chief Learning Officer,* and *CNBC.* She is a teaching faculty member of the Georgetown University Institute for Transformational Leadership.

Kristi lives in the Washington, D.C. area with her husband and two children.

For additional tools and resources, to stay in touch, and for more information about Kristi's executive coaching, keynotes, or group workshops, please visit:

Corporate site: thehedgescompany.com
Blog: kristihedges.com
Facebook: facebook.com/powerofpresence
Twitter: @kristihedges